Rethinking
Human Nature

Rethinking Human Nature

A CHRISTIAN MATERIALIST
ALTERNATIVE TO
THE SOUL

KEVIN J. CORCORAN

Baker Academic
Grand Rapids, Michigan

© 2006 by Kevin J. Corcoran

Published by Baker Academic
a division of Baker Publishing Group
P.O. Box 6287, Grand Rapids, MI 49516-6287
www.bakeracademic.com

Printed in the United States of America

Library of Congress Cataloging-in-Publication Data
Corcoran, Kevin, 1964–
    Rethinking human nature : a Christian materialist alternative to the soul / Kevin J. Corcoran.
        p.   cm.
    Includes bibliographical references and index.
    ISBN 10: 0-8010-2780-2 (pbk.)
    ISBN 978-0-8010-2780-2 (pbk.)
    1. Philosophical anthropology. 2. Man (Christian theology). 3. Christianity—Philosophy. I. Title.
BD450.C635 2006
128—dc22
                                                                2005037188

In Memoriam
Patrick G. Corcoran
(1932–68),
the father I never got to know,
and
Samuel J. Baum
(1956–2004),
faithful friend, dearly loved

Contents

Acknowledgments   9

Introduction: What Kind of Things Are We?   11

1 Dualist Views of Human Persons   23

2 Nothing-But Materialism   47

3 The Constitution View   65

4 The Stem Cell Challenge   83

5 I Believe in the Resurrection of the Body and the Life of the World to Come   119

6 The Constitution View and the Bible: Some Final Thoughts   135

Index   149

Acknowledgments

I WISH TO ACKNOWLEDGE THE FOLLOWING journals and people for kindness and generosity. Parts of chapter 3 previously appeared as "Persons, Bodies, and the Constitution Relation," *Southern Journal of Philosophy* 37 (1999): 1–20. Part 1 of chapter 4 borrows heavily from my "Material Persons, Immaterial Souls, and an Ethic of Life," *Faith and Philosophy* 20 (2003): 218–28. Material in chapter 5 previously appeared as "Dualism, Materialism, and the Problem of Post Mortem Survival," *Philosophia Christi* 4 (2002): 395–409. I thank these journals for permission to include that material here.

Writing this book was made enormously pleasurable largely because it was written in conversation with people I know and love. Some of them (perhaps even most) do not agree with the view of human nature I defend in these pages. But all of them provided invaluable, generous assistance.

First, Steve and Susan Matheson provided exceptionally good, incisive feedback. Steve is a biologist and Calvin colleague, and he helped save me from making many errors in the discussion of embryology and stem cell research covered in chapter 4. Whatever errors remain in those sections exist in spite of Steve's best efforts. Susan read both an early and a penultimate draft of the entire manuscript and provided excellent feedback. Again, whatever deficiencies remain do so in spite of Susan's best efforts to help spare me embarrassment.

I thank, too, my good friend Ron Scheller, who, like Susan, is exactly the kind of reader I am aiming for in this book. Ron is not a professional philosopher or a theologian, but he has the virtue of being naturally inquisitive, and he enjoys a rigorous intellectual workout. His comments, objections, and criticisms on the material in chapter 4 were enormously helpful. Where I failed to heed the sober advice of Ron and Susan, it is probably my undoing.

Greg Ganssle is another good friend. Greg forced me to rethink, rearrange, and reconsider many of the matters I take up in these pages. It is truly no exaggeration to say that this book would be much the worse if not for Greg's helpful, fair, and often humorous feedback on the entire manuscript.

Thanks are also due to two anonymous readers who provided helpful feedback on the manuscript.

Finally, I thank my dear friend Samuel Baum, who discussed with me all the issues addressed in this book and lots more over the course of a seventeen-year friendship. Sam passed away before I could bring the book to completion.

Introduction

WHAT KIND OF THINGS ARE WE?

IN 1968, I LOST MY father to cancer. I was four years old. I can still remember the funeral home. And I can remember that as I looked into the casket my mother told me that my father was now with God in heaven. I remember being perplexed. And why not? For all appearances, my father was lying lifeless before me. How could he be with God in heaven? Now I understand that my mother believed what most Christians have believed down through the centuries, namely, that we human persons are *immaterial souls*. According to this view, my father's lifeless body may have been lying before me but not my father. For although we human persons may be contingently and tightly joined to human bodies during the course of our earthly existence, so the view goes, we can, and in fact one day will, exist without them.

During the final stages of writing this book, I lost a dear friend to a malevolent brain tumor. I watched as the tumor and the medications used to treat the tumor ravaged his body, stole his short-term memory, and radically altered his appearance and personality. The destruction was complete in a matter of months. Through much of his short illness, my friend and I explored together, as we had done for so many years, some of the more obvious possibilities concerning what we human persons most fundamentally are: We are immaterial souls; we are material bodies; we are a composite of immaterial soul and material body. We explored as well some not so obvious alternatives.

The topics we discussed—whether we human persons are or have immaterial souls capable of disembodied existence or whether we are merely human animals ultimately destined to dust—have long been topics of interest to professional philosophers, theologians, social scientists, and ethicists. But they have also been topics of interest to ordinary people—to four-year-old children trying to understand what happened to Daddy when Daddy is said to have died and to forty-eight-year-old computer programmers struggling to comprehend their quick and tragic disintegration.

Augustine (AD 354–430) and René Descartes (1596–1650) believed what my mother believes: that we are immaterial souls. My friend Sam, a man with a unique blend of Jewish and Eastern beliefs, believed something along these lines too. Despite a few dissenting voices, however, today the dominant view among professional philosophers, ethicists, neurobiologists, psychologists, and cognitive scientists is a "nothing but" version of materialism, the view that creatures like us are "nothing but" complicated neural networks or mere biological beasts.

The question of human nature ought to concern us all. Human cloning, tissue transplant therapies, stem cell research, and other genetic and reproductive technologies are reigniting debate about the issue of personhood and human nature and revealing the urgency and importance of careful thinking about the topic for ordinary people. Indeed, it is ordinary people who must make very practical, and often very gut-wrenching, beginning of life ethical decisions. Moreover, the question of human nature obviously touches on beliefs central to orthodox Christianity, such as belief in life after death and the claim that we human beings have been created in the image of God.

The central question addressed in the following pages, then, is the metaphysical question that Augustine ponders in book 7 of his *Confessions* and René Descartes poses in his *Meditations on First Philosophy*: What kind of thing am I?[1] Am I an immaterial thing or a material thing? Am I neither a soul nor a body but rather a

---

1. René Descartes, *Meditations on First Philosophy*, trans. Donald A. Cress, 3rd ed. (Indianapolis: Hackett, 1993). For the relationship between Augustianism and Cartesianism, see Stephen Menn, *Descartes and Augustine* (Cambridge: Cambridge University Press, 1998).

compound of the two? Are there alternatives to these views? In the pages to come, I tell you why I believe I am a material thing, even if the material thing I am is not—perhaps surprisingly—the biological body that constitutes me. In other words, I aim to say a good word on behalf of *materialism* about human persons,[2] and I am going to explain why I do this *precisely as* a Christian. Notice, I did not say I aim to say a good word on behalf of *nothing-but* materialism. That omission was intentional. I did not say that because I believe nothing-but materialism constitutes a false view of what we are. But materialism comes in varieties, just as dualism does. Therefore, I present a version of materialism that I believe appropriates the insights of both dualism and nothing-but materialism, without giving in to the excesses of either.

A LITTLE HISTORY

In AD 144, Marcion of Pontus (and later, Rome) was excommunicated from the church. There were several reasons for his excommunication. First, he rejected the Hebrew Scriptures, peddling instead his own scriptures, which consisted of a truncated version of the Gospel of Luke and ten Pauline epistles. Second, he had an outright contempt for the body and for all things material, going so far as to reject the doctrine of the incarnation on account of his antipathy for the body. Finally, and connected with his renunciation of the material, Marcion was excommunicated because the church believed he misunderstood Jesus' mission, seeing the coming of Jesus as involving the deliverance of humankind from the very world and bodies God had created and blessed but which Marcion proclaimed were the creations of a lesser god, a *demiurgus*, that the supreme God must overcome.[3]

In large part, therefore, the formation of the canon, the Christian Scripture, and the development of what would become the Apostles' Creed came about as the church's response to Marcion's

2. Notice that by materialism I mean materialism *about* human persons. I do not mean what philosophers mean by *philosophical naturalism*, the claim that what is physical exhausts what there is. Nor do I mean what many non-philosophers mean by materialism, namely, flagrant consumerism and hedonism.

3. See Alexander Roberts and James Donaldson, eds., *The Ante-Nicene Fathers*, vol. 3 (Grand Rapids: Eerdmans, 1950).

teachings. The creation of the canon signaled a rejection of Marcion's mutilated scriptures, and the Apostles' Creed spelled out the church's rejection of Marcion's flawed Christology, anthropology, and theology.

I call attention to this pivotal episode in the life of the church to highlight something important about embodiment. As Alan Verhey so eloquently states, "With respect to the body, not just the story Scripture tells but also the story the Christian community tells of Scripture is instructive for the Christian community."[4] The story of the formation of Christian Scripture and what would become the Apostles' Creed teaches us that the radical antimaterialism of Marcion has no place in the Christian community.

The Christian story, from the beginning of the narrative in Genesis to its dramatic climax in Revelation, is an "earthy" story, a story that celebrates materiality, laments its perversion by human sin, and eagerly awaits its ultimate glorification in the resurrection. It is the position of this book that a materialist view of human nature, as opposed to a dualist view, fits this earthy picture of the Bible's grand narrative most comfortably.

The main lineaments of the Christian story are familiar to those of us who understand ourselves and the world in their terms. In the beginning, God created. All things other than God were created by God. When God completed his work, God rested and proclaimed all things created *good*, even *very* good!

Note that there is, to be sure, a kind of dualism in the doctrine of creation, but it is not the kind of dualism that will occupy our attention in the coming pages. The kind of dualism embedded in the doctrine of creation is that between Creator and created, between God and that which is not God. *This* kind of dualism rules out two sorts of error. On the one hand, it rules out devotion to and idolatry of creation. On the other hand, it rules out antipathy toward and rejection of creation, including the human bodies God created. I am an avid supporter of this kind of dualism. The kind of dualism at issue in discussions of human nature, however, is a dualism of human body and immaterial soul, where human persons are either identified with an immaterial soul or have an immaterial soul attributed to them as an essential part. It is this

---

4. See Alan Verhey, *Reading the Bible in the Strange World of Medicine* (Grand Rapids: Eerdmans, 2003), 80.

latter kind of dualism that is the focus of our attention and the kind of dualism I reject.

But let's return to the Christian story. According to this story, the good creation sank into sin. Hence, its second chapter, so to speak, is that of the fall and terrestrial misery. Human disobedience resulted in a perverted and twisted creation. Nothing in creation emerged unscathed. But interestingly and thankfully, the response of the Creator was not to destroy all of creation and to forego material and terrestrial reality. Instead, God acted to restore and to redeem the material world he created and blessed. God did this, we Christians believe, ultimately by embodying himself and becoming incarnate in the flesh and bones of Jesus of Nazareth, the same Jesus who was resurrected and later glorified.

Therefore, from creation, through its fall and inaugural restoration, en route to its glorious consummation, the Christian story is, from start to finish, a story with embodiment as a central feature. In fact, the most prominent image used in Scripture for the eschaton is that of a great banquet, a eucharistic feast of carnal delight. Not a whiff of disembodied or ghostly existence is contained in that image.

The Christian story, with embodiment and incarnation at its center, provides the theological backdrop against which to measure our view of human nature. But when it comes to how person and body are related, most Christians are Platonists insofar as most think of themselves as an immaterial soul housed in a material body. Plato's Dualism, however, is not the only version of dualism. There is also Substance Dualism, Compound Dualism, and Emergent Dualism, and each offers an alternative to the dualism of Plato and the radical antimaterialism of Marcion.

A ROAD MAP

This book is organized in the following way. The first chapter examines three versions of dualism: Substance Dualism, Compound Dualism, and Emergent Dualism. What all these dualisms have in common is a belief that human beings are composed of immaterial souls, either in the sense of being identical with immaterial souls or in the sense of being a compound of immaterial souls and material bodies. Dualists are also committed to the belief that we can, in some sense, survive the death of our bodies. I point out the philosophical problems confronting these versions of dualism and argue that, although each is compatible with key Christian beliefs, they are nevertheless mistaken views of human nature.

In chapter 2 I examine the claim that we human persons are identical with our bodies. I consider two views people may mean to express with that claim and argue that neither view is true. One of the views discussed in this chapter is the view known as *animalism*. This view identifies human persons with human animals.[5] According to this view, you and I are *essentially* animals and only *contingently* persons, which is to say that while we could not exist and fail to be animals, we could exist (and in fact at one time did) without being persons. In other words, according to animalism, the property of being a person is like the property of being married or single. During some stages of our existence, we may be married, while during other stages of our existence, we may be single. During our fetal lives, we were *not* persons; now we are. If things should go badly for us, we may end up once again as nonpersons. For example, according to animalism, if the upper part of my brain should suffer traumatic damage, such that I completely lack all capacity for a psychological life, but the lower part of my brain remains intact, such that the biological functions necessary for biological life continue, then I should continue to exist (as an animal) but cease to be a person.

I will argue that there is an important sense in which it is true to say that we are human animals. Nevertheless, I argue that there is an equally important but different sense in which it is true to say that we are *not* human animals. The sense in which it is true to say that we are *not* animals is the sense in which it is true to say that we are not *identical* to our biological bodies. So, in this chapter I show why it is a mistake to identify human persons with human animals and, therefore, why I believe that animalism is false.

At the end of chapter 2, we find ourselves in a puzzling situation. For while I do not identify myself with an immaterial soul or a compound of soul and body, neither do I believe I am identical with the physical object that is my biological body. But how can that be? If I am not an immaterial soul or a compound of soul and body, how could I possibly be a material object if I am not the material object that is my body?

5. See Eric Olson, *The Human Animal: Personal Identity without Psychology* (New York: Oxford University Press, 1997); and Trenton Merricks, *Objects and Persons* (New York: Oxford University Press, 2001).

Chapter 3 seeks to explain what I realize sounds like an odd claim. The view I articulate in this chapter is known as the Constitution View.[6] According to it, we human persons are *constituted by* our bodies without being *identical with* the bodies that constitute us. To claim that human persons are constituted by bodies without being identical with the bodies that constitute them is not to make a special pleading for human persons. Lots of medium-sized material objects stand in constitution relations. For example, statues are often constituted by pieces of marble, copper, or bronze, but the statues are not *identical with* the pieces of marble, copper, or bronze that constitute them. Likewise, dollar bills, diplomas, and dust jackets are often constituted by pieces of paper, but none of those things is identical with the pieces of paper that constitute them. This chapter provides reasons why this is the case and, in particular, why human persons are constituted by, without being identical with, the material objects that constitute them.

Chapter 4 is in many ways the most important chapter, for one of the things that emerges in the course of chapter 3 causes many people (unnecessarily, I will argue) grave misgivings with respect to the Constitution View. It turns out, according to the Constitution View, that no early term human fetus constitutes a person. It also turns out that any entity once possessing but having lost all capacity for the relevant kinds of psychological states also fails to constitute a person. Therefore, some human organisms in so-called persistent vegetative states (PVS) no longer constitute persons. One important objection to the Constitution View, therefore, is that it has horrific ethical consequences, particularly at life's margins. And in this chapter I show why this objection is unfounded and how appropriation of key theological doctrines (such as the doctrines of creation, incarnation, and resurrection) offer the resources for mounting a strong case in favor of life.

In addition to ethical worries generated by the Constitution View, some think it is also ill equipped to deal with the afterlife. The criticism is usually put like this. Bodies peter out and eventually cease to exist. And according to the Constitution View, one's body is necessary

---

6. See my "Persons, Bodies, and the Constitution Relation," *Southern Journal of Philosophy* 37 (1999): 1–20; idem, "Persons and Bodies," *Faith and Philosophy* 15 (1998): 324–40; and idem, "A Constitution View of Persons," in *In Search of the Soul: Four Views of the Mind-Body Problem*, ed. Joel B. Green and Stuart L. Palmer (Downers Grove, IL: InterVarsity, 2005), 153–76.

(though not sufficient) for one's existence. How can a body that peters out and ceases to exist somehow turn up in the new Jerusalem? Worse, if the deceased *immediately* join the Savior in heaven, how can that fact be squared with the apparent fact that the corpse is often right before our eyes? Dualists do not have such problems to embarrass them, since immaterial souls are not subject to the vagaries of bodily demise.

In chapter 5 I argue that if the issue is simply one of postmortem survival then dualists do in fact have a much easier time accommodating such a doctrine. But if one is both a dualist and a *Christian*, then that person faces one of the same problems as a Christian materialist, namely, how to make sense of the Christian doctrine of the resurrection of the body. It is precisely that doctrine that needs to be addressed by Christians, dualists no less than materialists. Chapter 5 calls attention to the fact that none of the ecumenical creeds of the church confesses belief in a doctrine of soul survival. The Christian doctrine has been understood as the doctrine of bodily *resurrection*. Telling a story of how a body that apparently suffered a martyr's death can be numerically the same as a body that enjoys resurrection life, it turns out, is not the special preoccupation of twenty-first-century Christian materialists. This has been, at least until recently, a concern for dualists too.

The chapter thus provides an account of the resurrection that is compatible with both a doctrine of intermediate, conscious existence between death and resurrection and the belief that at death we cease to exist and come back into existence at some time in the future. The account also has the virtue of being neutral with respect to dualist and materialist views of human nature and can thus be embraced by dualists as well as materialists.

The sixth and final chapter rehearses the main lines of argument developed throughout the book and considers how the Constitution View developed in chapter 3 coheres with the biblical narrative concerning human nature. I suggest that the view coheres surprisingly well.

CHRISTIAN PHILOSOPHY

As a Christian, my philosophical work is informed by my Christian commitments. How? Let me sketch how I think about faith-informed scholarship and share with you why I believe this book is itself an instance of such scholarship. First, my Christian beliefs fall on an expanding series of concentric circles. In the center circle are the doctrines that form the substance of the ancient creeds of the church: the Nicene, the Apostolic, and the Athanasian.[7] These doctrines include the following: God is one yet triune; the Second Person of the Trinity became incarnate of the Virgin Mary and was made human; the incarnate Christ suffered, died, was buried, and rose again for the reconciliation of the world; the risen Christ will come again to judge the living and the dead; and we human beings will one day be raised in glory. Other beliefs reside in this center circle also, beliefs having to do with the Holy Spirit, the church, and so on. The beliefs that fall within the center are *essential* to Christian orthodoxy. To deny one of these doctrines is, I believe, to situate oneself outside the pale of orthodox Christian belief.[8]

Moving out from the center are other important Christian beliefs. For example, I have beliefs about infant baptism, what actually transpires in the celebration of the Eucharist, whether there are so-called second chances for reconciliation beyond the grave, whether God created human beings via natural processes or whether human beings are the result of "special" creation, and so on. These beliefs, important though they are, are not in the center of the series of concentric circles. They are, instead, somewhere outside the center moving toward the periphery of the series of circles. As I see it, they are not essential to orthodox Christian belief.

The doctrines that are located in the center circle function as constraints for me as a philosopher insofar as they circumscribe a range of possible answers and solutions to some of the questions I ask as a philosopher. For example, in the center of the series of concentric circles is the belief that though we human beings die yet shall we live. This belief serves as a defeater for any view of human nature that is incompatible with that doctrine. Since it seems to me that the two dominant views of human nature—dualism and animalism—are inadequate accounts of human nature, I have in these pages sought an

7. I am tempted to call these creeds the *ecumenical* creeds. However, strictly speaking, only the Nicene Creed is embraced by all three major branches of the Christian church, the Roman Catholic, Protestant, and Eastern Orthodox.

8. Although what I say here is, strictly speaking, true, there is nevertheless the following caveat. In the early ninth century, the Western Christian church added to the Nicene Creed the following concerning the Holy Spirit: "who proceeds from the Father and the Son." The Eastern church, of course, did not accept this addition, and the Christian church has been forever split as a result. For interesting reading on this matter, see Timothy Ware, *The Orthodox Church* (London: Penguin Books, 1997).

alternative. The Constitution View, developed in chapter 3, is a viable alternative for Christians insofar as it is perfectly compatible with those doctrines that fall within the center of the series of concentric circles into which Christian doctrines fall.

Not only do the beliefs that fall within the center circle function as potential defeaters for the philosophical views I entertain, but as a Christian scholar, my philosophical work is also shaped by and answerable to the larger Christian tradition. I work not in isolation, nor autonomously, but rather within the context of the wider Christian community, a community that includes not just the saints now living but also those faithful brothers and sisters who have gone before me and who have thought diligently and with integrity about some of the same issues I think about as a twenty-first-century Christian philosopher. Therefore, even if a particular belief of mine does not fall within the center of the series of concentric circles described a moment ago, but the belief has nevertheless held a prominent place among the Christian community throughout history, then to depart from history with respect to that belief requires explanation. It requires explanation insofar as the holder of the belief situates himself or herself within the community.

So, for example, a dualist view of human nature has been the majority view of Christians throughout the history of the church. The Constitution View, which I develop, entails the denial of dualism. Therefore, I owe the community an explanation as to why I see fit to depart from tradition by embracing a view that has not been endorsed by the majority of Christian thinkers throughout the centuries. I offer, therefore, the following principle for adopting beliefs that depart from tradition, beliefs that though important are nevertheless not essential to Christian orthodoxy.

The principle can be stated as follows. If on careful and thoughtful reflection it seems to me that a belief that is not central to ecumenical Christian orthodoxy, but has nevertheless held a prominent place within that tradition, is false *and* I can offer a plausible account of how the tradition may have come to that belief, then it is permissible for me to humbly, and with fear and trembling, depart from tradition with respect to that belief. With respect to dualism, I believe that the only way the church could articulate what makes us human persons unique among the natural creation was to introduce the existence of a soul. Like us, I believe that the early church fathers reasoned as follows: Either we are unique in creation, or we are not. If we are unique among creation, then we are not animals. If we are not identical with animals, then we either are or have immaterial souls. I will argue, however, that the Constitution View offers an account of human nature according to which we are unique among creation (we are *persons*) but not in virtue of possessing an immaterial soul. Finally, on the issue of faith-informed scholarship, let me add this. Discussion is to Christian philosophy what lab work is to the practice of biology. We cannot have the one without the other. As a Christian philosopher, I must answer not only to my Christian brothers and sisters who are also philosophers, and who disagree with me, but also to those of my brothers and sisters who are not philosophers. For all I know, one day I may come to regard the view I hold on the metaphysical nature of human beings as flawed beyond repair and come instead to embrace a version of dualism. For now, it seems to me that the Constitution View offers a plausible alternative to the two major accounts of human nature. The burden of this book is to make a case for that claim.

AUDIENCE

This book is aimed at two audiences. On the one hand, it is aimed at students of philosophy and theology interested in the current debate surrounding human nature. While I hope that professional philosophers and theologians who keep up with discussions in the latest professional journals might find something useful in these pages too, such philosophers and theologians are not my primary aim. The other audience I am interested in reaching is the audience of inquisitive and intelligent lay persons interested in the issues taken up in these pages. To this audience, I make no apology for the level of intellectual energy the following chapters require. Reading this book will not be like passively watching a television show. I take for granted a reader who is first of all interested in the issues addressed here and who also finds a fairly rigorous intellectual workout something of a pleasure.

A CONFESSION

We are almost ready to jump in, but before we get started, I want to make a few things clear. First, in rejecting dualism, I am not rejecting the claim that we human persons are created in the image of God, nor am I rejecting the claim that something sets us apart from the rest of nature. I am rejecting only the claim that we are identical with, or partly composed of, an immaterial substance.

Second, considering things like the doctrine of the resurrection and the metaphysical nature of human persons is difficult business. Despite what some may claim, whatever the truth regarding these issues, it is not transparent and obvious. Even so, some philosophers are prepared to speak in bold and authoritative terms. I myself am hesitant to speak in such a way. I have thought long and hard about these matters and am committed to the truth of the views I hold. However, it is conceivable that I should one day learn, perhaps in heaven, and certainly to my chagrin, that not my view but one of the views I reject is the truth about our nature. Then I should be like the ancient Greek astronomer Ptolemy, who did his level best to seek the truth and weigh the evidence about the heavenly bodies but whom, for all of that, was nevertheless mistaken in his geocentric view of the universe.

This book, therefore, is not offered in the hope of providing the final word on the issues it entertains. It is not even offered as the final thoughts of its author. It is, rather, offered in the hope of stimulating further debate and reflection on the age-old question of human nature and the important, contemporary ethical issues of stem cell research and human cloning. Like all views on issues of fundamental human concern, what I say in these pages is open to criticism, correction, and revision.

I

Dualist Views of Human Persons

THIS CHAPTER CONSIDERS THREE VERSIONS of dualism
and explores the various reasons and arguments that have been
offered in their defense. I will suggest that none of the versions, or
the arguments offered in their defense, is ultimately persuasive. In
the next chapter, I consider animalism, the most obvious alternative
to dualism.

SUBSTANCE DUALISM: PLATO (427–347 BC)

Plato, ancient Athenian philosopher and student of Socrates, offered some interesting even if, from our vantage point in history,
odd reasons for believing that, unlike our material bodies, we are
immortal. In his work the *Phaedo*, for example, Plato offered as one
reason for believing that we are immortal the claim that all knowledge
is a recollection of things forgotten, due to our embodiment. If all
knowledge is a form of recollection of things forgotten because of
embodiment, then we must have known things *before* our embodiment. Therefore, unlike our bodies, we are immortal.[1]

1. See Plato, *Phaedo* in *Five Dialogues*, trans. G. M. A. Grube (Indianapolis and
Cambridge: Hackett, 1981).

To argue for our immortality, however, is not the same as establishing that we are immaterial souls. But adding a few more premises can secure the Platonic claim for immateriality. For example, if our bodies are mortal and we are not, then quite obviously we are not our bodies, at least not according to the plausible assumption that a single thing cannot both be and not be mortal. If human bodies are mortal because they are material, but we ourselves are immortal, then we must be immaterial. Indeed, Plato's view was precisely that: We are immaterial souls, relating to our bodies in roughly the same way that a hand relates to a glove. Here then is one way to state Plato's claims about immortality.

First Stage Argument

1. Human persons are immortal.
2. Human bodies are not immortal.
3. One thing cannot both be and not be mortal.
4. Therefore, human persons are not human bodies.

Second Stage Argument

5. Human bodies are material things.
6. No material thing is immortal.
7. Human persons are immortal.
8. Therefore, human persons are not material things.

These are good arguments in the sense that they are what philosophers call deductively valid arguments (i.e., their form or structure is such that if all the premises are true, then the conclusions *must* be true). Here is another way of putting it: Good deductive arguments are such that it is not possible for all the premises to be true and the conclusions to be false. However, deductive validity is one thing; deductive *soundness* is another. The ultimately important question is whether the arguments are sound. Deductively sound arguments are such that they are (1) valid and (2) all their premises are in fact true. So the question is, Are all the premises of the arguments true?

As Christians, we have good reason to reject the first premise of the first stage argument and premise 7 of the second stage argument. Although we believe we will exist after death, the Christian tradition does not assert either that we existed *prior* to our embodiment or that we are *naturally* immortal (i.e., that living forever is a part of human nature independent of God's divine intervention). Indeed, the Christian tradition denounced the claim of natural immortality as heresy at the fifth ecumenical council (the Second Constantinople Council in AD 553). Based solely on this observation, a Christian has reason to conclude that these Plato-inspired arguments are not sound. In other words, these arguments do not succeed in establishing that we are immaterial souls.

The fact that these arguments do not succeed in establishing the truth of the Platonic conclusion does not mean, however, that the conclusion is not true. Maybe we *are* immaterial things, as Plato claimed, but these particular arguments fail to establish that we are. Let us therefore consider other, perhaps more successful, arguments for dualism.

SUBSTANCE DUALISM: RENÉ DESCARTES (1596–1650)

René Descartes is a much maligned philosopher among the educated elite of the twenty-first century, primarily because of his mechanistic view of nature and his old-fashioned (and, according to current trends, unfashionable) mind-body or person-body dualism. Many in the academy hold Cartesianism responsible for everything from the oppression of women to the degradation of the human body and the pillaging of the environment. Even some professional philosophers think they can dismiss Descartes with a mere wave of the hand, believing his Substance Dualism unworthy of a serious hearing in these days of enlightened thinking.

At the end of the day, I think Descartes is mistaken in his view of human nature; nevertheless, it is wrong to believe that we can refute his dualism simply by wrinkling our nose at it. Descartes had reasons and arguments for believing what he did. Those reasons and arguments need to be taken seriously. Indeed, one of the greatest compliments we can pay important thinkers now dead is to treat them as conversation partners, behaving as though they were sitting right across the table from us discussing matters of deep and abiding significance. We may disagree with them, but let them have their say. And if we are going to reject their views, we need to do so not on the basis of what is trendy but on the basis of good reasons.[2]

In a nutshell, the Cartesian view of human nature is as follows: Human bodies are unthinking, spatially extended things (i.e., they are spread out in space). They are quite ordinary physical objects composed of ordinary matter in complex configurations. Since they are unthinking, they have no mental or psychological properties. Human persons or souls, on the other hand, are spatially unextended, thinking things. They are nonphysical and as such have no mass or physical location. Souls think, experience pleasure and pain, set goals, and act to accomplish them. When body and soul are functioning together properly, one soul will interact with a single body, and *that* body will provide *that* soul with sensory input, which the soul will utilize in various mental tasks. Souls but not bodies are specially created by God.

Let us now examine Descartes's reasons for believing that soul and body are two distinct kinds of things.

The Initial Argument

One of Descartes's fundamental intuitions was that the world is divided at a primary level between substances and properties. It is helpful to think of substances as *things* and properties as the ways things can be or fail to be. For example, being green, weighing two tons, and being six feet tall are all ways things can be or, in my case, fail to be. (I am not green, do not weigh two tons, and am not six feet tall.) The Cartesian intuition is that properties are all like headaches in the sense that we will never find a headache just hanging out without anyone having it. Headaches are necessarily *had*. Likewise,

2. As for dualism's responsibility for the oppression of women, the degradation of the human body, and the pillaging of the environment, such social ills are connected to dualism only by historical accident and are nothing like logical entailments of dualism. In other words, there is nothing logically inconsistent with a Cartesian Dualist being a fierce defender of gender equity and an enthusiastic supporter of environmental causes. A profound sense of stewardship, the belief that our bodies and the environment are not our own but belong to God, who has certain aims and intentions for them, is sufficient to underwrite an ethic of care for the body and the environment. A corresponding belief that women are created in God's image and variably gifted no less and no different from men is sufficient to motivate gender equity on the part of a dualist. Therefore, the assertion that dualism is responsible for nearly all the social ills we face is really quite without warrant.

we will not find colors or weights or heights without things that are colored, have a certain weight, or have a certain height. So, there are properties, and there are the things that have them, substances.

Descartes used this basic, commonsense intuition to argue that persons and bodies are distinct kinds of things or substances. He noted that properties themselves are divided into two kinds, those that are mental (e.g., being in pain, desiring an ice-cream cone, or hoping that the Orioles have a winning season this year) and those that are physical (e.g., having a certain weight, shape, and mass). Descartes, in other words, was a dualist about properties (some are mental, and some are physical). What Cartesian Dualism adds to Property Dualism is a claim about substance. The claim is that a single kind of thing can have properties of only one sort. Therefore, a Cartesian Dualist claims that there must be two fundamental kinds of substance—spatially unextended, thinking substance (soul or person) and unthinking, spatially extended substance (body). The appropriate bearers of mental properties are unextended, thinking substances (souls or persons), and the appropriate bearers of physical properties are unthinking, extended substances (bodies). Descartes famously argued that he is essentially a thinking thing. If that is so, then Descartes is an immaterial soul or mind.

Here is Descartes's argument laid out in logical form:

Assumption: Properties are necessarily had or owned.

1. There are two kinds of properties (mental/thinking and material/nonthinking).
2. A single thing can have properties of only one sort.
3. Therefore, there are two kinds of substances (mental and material).
4. I am essentially a thinking substance.
5. Therefore, I am a mental (i.e., immaterial) substance.

This is a beautiful argument, and it will not do as a refutation just to assert that it is passé and unenlightened. If we're going to reject the argument, we're going to have to do better than that. Let me add, however, before moving on, that according to Descartes's view, although it is true of me now that I am in some sense inextricably bound up with this particular body, my existence does not depend on my possessing either this or any other body (i.e., I could exist in

a disembodied state). Why did Descartes think that? According to
Descartes, the fundamentally dissimilar natures of souls and bodies
account for this. There is, for example, nothing in the nature of soul
that requires for its existence the existence of a body. Nor is there
anything in the nature of body that requires for its existence the existence of a soul or mind. To be a soul is to be simple, unextended, and
thinking. To be a body is to be complex, extended, and unthinking.
Thus, Descartes reckoned it *possible* for the one kind of substance to
exist without the other, and the other to exist without the one. Since
Descartes was a Christian, be believed that God would actualize that
possibility at the appointed time.

There is a problem here, however. Let's step back a moment.
Descartes's argument depends on the claim that a single thing can
have properties of only one kind, mental or physical, but not both.
Well, why not both? Why couldn't a single thing have both mental
properties and physical properties? More specifically, why couldn't
a *physical* thing have *mental* properties? Descartes cannot just assert
the impossibility. He must give good reasons for thinking it is true.
He does not. Nor has anyone since Descartes succeeded in showing
why a physical thing cannot have both kinds of properties. Therefore,
this initial argument has not succeeded in proving that Descartes is
an immaterial soul.

The Separability Argument

Even if one were to grant the objection above, other arguments
of Descartes must be considered. Indeed, in his *Meditations on First
Philosophy*, he presents two arguments for what he calls "the real
distinction" between a person and a body. The first argument is the
separability argument. In this argument, Descartes claims that if he can
clearly and distinctly conceive of one thing existing without another
thing existing, then the two are distinct things. He goes on to claim
that he can conceive of himself existing without his body existing.
He concludes, therefore, that he is one thing and his body is another,
different thing. Of course, Descartes does not believe he is special in
this regard. If *he* is an immaterial soul, then so are you.

I like this argument. Since one thing cannot exist without existing,
it must be true that *if* I can exist without my body existing, then I
am one thing and my body is a different thing. Right? Think about
it this way: Can you conceive of your church existing without your

church building existing? If so, then your church is not identical with your church building. Your church is one thing, and your church building is another thing altogether. Just as you can conceive of your church existing without your church building existing, so Descartes can conceive of himself existing without his body existing. Let's put it like this:

1. If I can clearly and distinctly conceive of one thing existing without another thing existing, then the two are distinct things.
2. I can clearly and distinctly conceive of myself existing without my body existing.
3. Therefore, I am not the same thing as my body and can exist without it.

Again, this is a valid argument: If all the premises are true, then the conclusion must be true as well. Are all the premises true? There are good reasons for calling into question the truth of premise 2. First, Descartes must provide some way of distinguishing *genuine* clear and distinct conceptions from *apparent* clear and distinct conceptions. After all, it sometimes seems to us that we are clearly and distinctly conceiving something when, in actuality, we are not.

Here is an interesting example. Can you conceive of Saul of Tarsus, that scoundrel, persecutor of Christians, existing without the apostle Paul, that faithful disciple of Jesus, existing? You may think you can conceive of this. After all, you can conceive of Saul never having met Jesus on the Damascus road, and therefore, of Paul never having existed. Actually, however, you cannot possibly conceive of Saul existing without Paul existing or vice versa. Why? Because Saul is Paul (i.e., Saul and Paul are *numerically identical*). "They" are the same person. One guy, two names.

But didn't we just say that we could conceive of Saul never having met Jesus on the road to Damascus? Yes, we did. But that is not to conceive of Saul existing without Paul existing. That is just to conceive of Saul (Paul) never having had a certain experience. Consider the following: Can you conceive of Samuel Clemens never having written *Huckleberry Finn*? Sure. But that is not to conceive of Samuel Clemens existing without Mark Twain existing. Samuel Clemens *is* Mark Twain. And, one thing cannot exist without existing.

Therefore, even though it may seem we are conceiving something, we may not be. Descartes needs to give us some reason for believing that he is not making the same sort of mistake in his second premise as someone is making who claims to conceive of Saul existing without Paul existing or Cassius Clay existing without Mohamed Ali existing. He gives no such reasons. His failure in this respect gives us reason to call into question the truth of his second premise and therefore the soundness of his separability argument.[3]

Before moving on, let me say something about our intuitions concerning Saul and Paul. What accounts for the fact that we believe (falsely) that we can conceive of the one existing without the other existing is the fact that outside philosophy we use the term *identical* or the phrase *the same as* in a loose and nontechnical sense. We might say, for example, that your book is "the same as" mine or that we have "identical" computers. What we mean is that our books or computers are *phenomenologically indistinguishable* (they look exactly alike). When philosophers use the term *identical* or the phrase *the same as*, they do *not* have in mind phenomenological similarity. Instead, they are thinking in terms of number, the number one. With respect to number, of course, you and I do not have the same book or the same computer. You have one, and I have one, and one plus one makes two. The distinction between *numerical* sameness and what we might call *qualitative* sameness leads me to say that Saul is Paul. Saul and Paul are not *two* persons but one.

When I use the example of Saul and Paul with my students, they usually protest: "But we can conceive of Saul never having met Jesus on the road to Damascus. If so, Paul never would have existed, but Saul would have. So Saul is *not* Paul." "Plus," they say, "didn't Paul say in 2 Corinthians 5:17 that if anyone is in Christ they are a new creature; the old has passed away, behold the new has come?" As I have said, this much is certainly true: Saul may never have met Jesus on the Damascus road, and Paul is a new creature in Christ. What is *not* true is that Saul could have existed without Paul (or vice versa) or that at some time on the Damascus road one person (Saul) ceased to exist and a numerically distinct person (Paul) replaced him. Think about it this way. Did Paul experience a conversion? Certainly he did, one of the most spectacular conversions in history. If there is a conversion, then there must be a *single* thing that survives or undergoes

---

3. Since Descartes is providing an argument *for* Substance Dualism, the onus of responsibility is on him to make the case that he is not making the kind of mistake I claim he *might* be making. The onus of responsibility is not on a materialist to make the case that Descartes *is*, in fact, making such a mistake.

the conversion. There must be a single thing that radically changes. To say "I am a completely different person since I met Christ" is to say that I was once one way and now I—the self same I—am quite a different way. Therefore, in the *numerical* sense, Saul *is* Paul (there is just *one* guy), but that one guy has radically changed.[4] It is not that God annihilated one person (Saul) and replaced him with a numerically distinct person (Paul). There is *one* guy in the story, and his life has been radically altered. The same point about numerical sameness could be made by using Cassius Clay and Mohammed Ali, Samuel Clemens and Mark Twain, or Clark Kent and Superman. In each case, a *single* individual goes by different names. In the first and last cases, the different names signal a radical change in the individual, just as is often assumed to be the case with Saul/Paul.

Again, Descartes must make the case that he is not making this kind of mistake. If Descartes is identical to his body, then he cannot possibly conceive of himself existing without his body existing. Why? Because a single thing cannot exist without existing. On the basis of this criticism alone, we must conclude that there are problems with Descartes's separability argument. In other words, Descartes has not succeeded in proving that he is one thing and his body is a different thing.

The Divisibility Argument

Even if I am correct in my critique of Descartes's separability argument, Descartes has another argument for the same dualist conclusion. This argument concerns the divisibility of bodies and the indivisibility of minds or souls. Here is the argument:

1. Bodies are divisible into parts.
2. Souls are not divisible into parts.
3. The same thing cannot both be and not be divisible into parts.
4. Therefore, souls and bodies are distinct things.

First, a point of clarity. By "bodies," Descartes does not have in mind only physical objects like those we use to walk to the store,

---

4. It was, I am told, the custom for Jewish people in the diaspora to have two names—one Jewish and the other Greek/Roman. Therefore, the Saul/Paul problem, as I have set it up, assumes the mistaken view that the two names track the pre- and post-Christ experience of Paul (Saul). Even so, you get the point.

pick up a baseball, or bump a car door shut. A body is any spatially extended thing. Therefore, the computer I am typing on is, in this sense, a body, as is a carrot, a combustion engine, or even a carnation. Each is a body, and each is divisible into parts.

It is important to note, too, that Descartes does not just help himself to premises 1 and 2. He has arguments for those too. For example, Descartes notes that bodies are extended in space (i.e., they are spread out). Extended things are divisible into parts. Therefore, Descartes concludes that bodies are divisible into parts. So far so good. Descartes's reasoning for the second premise is more nuanced. He does not reason that since souls are *not extended* in space they are, therefore, not divisible into parts. Instead, he reasons that if souls *were* divisible into parts he should be able to conceive of dividing them into parts. But Descartes cannot conceive of dividing souls or minds into parts; therefore, he concludes that minds or souls are not divisible into parts. That gives Descartes his second premise. The third premise needs no argument. It is self-evidently true.

This argument, like those preceding it, is deductively valid: If all its premises are true, then the conclusion must be true. Are all its premises true? The first premise seems true. Even if a body were so small that one could not, physically, divide it into parts, we could conceive of its right and left sides, or its top and its bottom. So let's give Descartes the first premise: Bodies are divisible into parts.

What about Descartes's second premise? Here we run into the problem with the argument. Does it follow from Descartes's inability to conceive of dividing a mind into parts that minds or souls are not divisible into parts? I don't think so. Descartes's inability to conceive of dividing a mind into parts may just signal a limitation on what Descartes can conceive, not what can or cannot be divided into parts. Consider the following example. To casual observation, a physical object like a table appears stable and unitary. However, if what physicists tell us is true, the true nature of the table is not like that. It is, in fact, composed of many tiny things in rapid motion. What gives the table the appearance of stability is the rapid motion of the atoms, their lattice structure, and the repulsion behavior of electrons. The point is that the actual nature of the table is not transparent to casual observation. In the same way, perhaps the mind or soul is divisible, but this fact is simply not transparent to Cartesian introspection. Just as we cannot tell the true nature of a table simply by looking at it, so too, perhaps, we cannot tell that minds or souls are divisible just through introspection. Perhaps we need a neuroscientist to reveal to us the divisibility of the mind.

In short, from Descartes's inability to conceive of dividing the mind, it does not follow that the mind or soul is not divisible. Yet without the truth of that premise, Descartes's divisibility argument for the distinction between a person and his or her body fails.

Taken together we have good reasons for believing that Descartes failed to prove what he set out to prove, namely, that we are one thing and our bodies are numerically distinct things of an altogether different kind. Granted, Descartes's conclusion could be true, even if he failed to prove it, but we must admit that so far we have not been given ultimately persuasive reasons for believing that conclusion. Without ultimately persuasive reasons for believing it, we should withhold our assent to the Cartesian claim that we are immaterial souls.

The Simple Argument

There is one final kind of argument for Substance Dualism to consider, and it is the simple argument. It is as follows:

1. I am essentially simple.
2. My body is essentially complex.
3. If I am identical with my body, then whatever is a property of the one is a property of the other and vice versa.
4. Because I have an essential property that my body lacks, I am not identical with my body.[5]

It would be a mistake to embrace Substance Dualism on account of this argument. The reason is that, perhaps surprisingly, the simple argument is not an argument for Substance Dualism. It is, rather, an argument for the conclusion that one is not identical with one's body. And one need not be a dualist to believe that one is not identical with one's body. I, for example, think the conclusion of the simplicity argument is true.[6] Yet I think the argument is unsound, owing to the

5. See Stewart Goetz, "Substance Dualism," in *In Search of the Soul: Four Views of the Mind-Body Problem*, ed. Joel B. Green and Stuart L. Palmer (Downers Grove, IL: InterVarsity, 2005), 33–60.

6. If each occurrence of the English word *I* in the simplicity argument is read as "the immaterial soul that is me," then I could not endorse the conclusion, and my criticism would fail, for then the conclusion comes to "because the immaterial soul that is me

falsity of premise 1. Here is what I take to be a sound argument to the same conclusion as the simplicity argument:

1. I am essentially a psychological being.
2. My body is not essentially a psychological being.
3. A single thing cannot both be and not be an essentially psychological being.
4. Therefore, I am not identical with my body.

Again, this is not an argument *for* Substance Dualism. It is an argument whose conclusion is compatible with *both* dualism and certain versions of physicalism. For example, it is consistent with the Constitution View presented in chapter 3. Even more surprising than the fact that the simplicity argument is not an argument for dualism is the fact that one could grant the truth of *all* the premises of the simplicity argument, and so commit oneself to the conclusion, without embracing dualism or the Constitution View, for one could insist that one is identical with a *physically* simple object, such as a partless atom in one's brain.

PROBLEMS FOR SUBSTANCE DUALISM

As I see it, none of the arguments for Substance Dualism we have considered succeeds. Descartes's arguments do not succeed, nor does the simple argument. There are, however, other reasons independent of the failure of Descartes's arguments and the simple argument for calling into question Substance Dualism. For example, advances in brain science suggest that the mind is causally dependent on the brain for its existence and functioning in ways that we simply would not expect if Substance Dualism were true. Consciousness itself, for example, can be altered or even (apparently) extinguished by tinkering with certain regions of the brain via drugs or more direct means. Moreover, Descartes is infamous for his belief that only human animals are endowed with soul and so with mental lives. Nonhuman animals lack soul and so lack a corresponding mental life; they are

---

has an essential property my body lacks, the immaterial soul that is me is not identical with my body." And it does seem that one cannot embrace *that* conclusion without also embracing dualism. Of course, if that is how "I" is to be understood throughout the argument, then the argument seems to me to be completely unmotivated.

mere machines. But this notion seems to be refuted by anyone who has ever owned or spent time with a dog or a cat, for dogs and cats seem quite clearly to have some degree or level of a mental life. If they do, then one begins to wonder whether birds, bees, and bullfrogs also have mental lives, though, quite obviously, mental lives not equal to that of dogs, cats, or humans in terms of power and ability. But if nonhuman animals enjoy mental lives too, then what distinguishes human from nonhuman animals is not the presence of a soul.

I have said why I do not find any of the arguments offered on behalf of Substance Dualism persuasive, and I have also suggested some reasons why one may think Substance Dualism faces some problems. However, I have not offered a philosophical argument for why I believe Substance Dualism is false. Truth be known, of course, there is no argument I can give that is valid and has premises that both dualists and materialists will grant. Even so, there is one argument I take to be decisive against the claim that I am a Cartesian, simple soul. Here it is:

1. I sometimes kiss my wife.
2. My substantively simple soul never kisses anyone (it has no lips).
3. Therefore, I am not a simple soul.[7]

Surprising though it is, not even this gem of an argument is found persuasive by Cartesian Dualists. Perhaps at this point, we should turn our attention to other versions of dualism that may fare better than Descartes's.

COMPOUND DUALISM: THOMAS AQUINAS (1225–74)

As we have seen, according to both the Platonic view and the Cartesian view of human nature, human persons are immaterial souls. Such a view is flatly rejected by Compound Dualists. The most intuitive way to express this view is to say that, while there are souls and there are bodies, we human persons are neither a soul nor a body. We are what you get when a soul and a body are joined together.

7. This argument is brazenly borrowed from a conversation with Trenton Merricks.

Although that is the most intuitive way of putting it, a more careful presentation of the view is provided by Thomas Aquinas.[8] Aquinas claimed that human persons are, in some sense, *material* beings and *not* identical with immaterial souls, even though human persons are *partly* composed of immaterial souls.

Like Aristotle, Aquinas held that all material objects are form-matter composites. In other words, material objects are *compound* objects, a combination of form and matter. Human persons, Aquinas believed, share with all other material objects this feature of having both matter and form. The soul, Aquinas would say, is the *substantial form* of a human person. That is to say, the soul is that which makes a particular material thing a *human* being and not some other kind of thing.[9]

We must be careful, however, not to think of the soul or the substantial form of a thing merely as its shape. Rather, for Aquinas, the substantial form of a thing is dynamic insofar as it concerns the *arrangement* of material parts of a thing together with their properties *and* the causal relations those parts stand in to one another. So, for example, Aquinas did not believe that the corpse left behind after an ordinary death of a human being is a *dead* human being. It is not a human being at all. Instead, death marks the replacement of one kind of form with another.

According to Aquinas's Compound Dualist view, a human soul is a kind of form, and forms are dynamic states. Souls are immaterial, but given his rejection of a Cartesian sort of dualism, he did not identify

8. I say "more careful" because Aquinas would not say that souls and bodies are independently existing substances that are joined together. This makes both soul and body appear too much like Cartesian substances. Aquinas's view is much more nuanced than that. In what follows, I attempt to capture some of that nuance. However, I direct the reader to the following in-depth treatments of Aquinas on human nature: Eleonore Stump, "Non-Cartesian Substance Dualism and Materialism without Reductionism," *Faith and Philosophy* 12 (1995): 505–31; and more recently, Robert Pasnau, *Thomas Aquinas on Human Nature: A Philosophical Study of Summa Theologiae 1a, 75–89* (New York: Cambridge University Press, 2002).

9. Of course, Aquinas also believes that all plants and nonhuman animals have souls. Plants have souls in virtue of their capacity for nutrition, growth, reproduction, etc., those activities common to living things. Nonhuman animals have souls in virtue of having those same capacities. But the souls of nonhuman animals are also such that they have the capacity for perception. What is unique about humans is that in addition to the capacities already mentioned, humans have the capacity for intellective functioning. For further discussion of this point, see Stump, "Non-Cartesian Substance Dualism," 509.

a human person with his or her soul. Rather, a human person is a soul-body composite.

COMPOUND DUALISM: SUBSTANCE DUALISM AFTER ALL?

Anyone familiar with Aquinas's metaphysics of material substance must admit that his view of human nature is in tension with his metaphysics of material substance. For example, Aquinas believed that human souls survive the disintegration of the soul-body composite. But how can that be? Presumably, as a configurational or dynamic state, the soul must configure or be a state *of* something. But it seems that after death there is nothing left for the soul to configure or be a state of. If a separated soul is a state, then presumably it is a state *of* something. But of what?

Eleonore Stump explains this puzzling feature of Aquinas's view. She says that, for Aquinas, "to be is to be configured or to have a form."[10] Thus, God and the angels, according to Aquinas's view, have form even if no matter. God's being configured amounts to the fact that God is a kind of thing with one rather than another set of properties. Anything that has order and species is configured or has form. Therefore, God has form. The idea is this. There are some forms that configure something, and there are other forms that do not configure something else but are themselves configured (e.g., angels). Therefore, according to Stump, "it is possible for something to be both configured and a configurer of other things."[11] Such things are, in Stump's language, configured configurers. Here is Stump:

> The metaphysical world is ordered in such a way that at the top of the metaphysical hierarchy there are forms—God and the angels—which are configured but which aren't configurational constituents of anything else. These forms are configured but non-configuring. Near the bottom of the hierarchy are forms that configure matter but don't exist as configured things in their own right. The form of an amethyst is like this. . . . And in the middle are human souls, the amphibians of this metaphysical world, occupying a niche in both the material

10. Ibid., 513.
11. Ibid., 514. Stump considers a particular kind of protein (CAT/Enhancer Binding Protein). Such proteins are configured molecules with the capacity to configure other molecules.

and the spiritual realm. . . . The human soul, then, is a configured configurer.[12]

If this is how we are to understand Aquinas, then don't we land square in the Substance Dualist camp once again? Stump and others are right to point out that such is not the case. First, a Substance Dualist (like Descartes) claims that both the soul and the body are *substances* in their own right. Each is capable of acting independently of the other, and each can causally interact with the other. Moreover, it is possible that the soul of a human person, according to Cartesian Substance Dualism, is separable and can engage in thinking and other mental acts quite independent of embodiment and on their own. Compound Dualists like Aquinas, on the other hand, reject both these claims.

According to Aquinas, although the human soul can exist after death, it is not a substance "in its own right." How so? Aquinas held that two kinds of things can exist on their own: complete substances and subsistents (things that can exist on their own but are not complete substances, such as a hand or a foot).[13] Souls are incomplete substances. Aquinas states:

> Not every particular substance is a hypostasis or a person . . . but [only] that which has the complete nature of the species. So a hand or a foot cannot be called a hypostasis or person, and similarly, neither can the soul, since it is [only] a part [of a complete human being].[14]

So, according to Aquinas, or Compound Dualism, "body and soul are not two actually existing substances; instead, one actually existing substance arises from these two."[15] Here is one way to mark the difference between Aquinas and Descartes. In both views, there are two "things." In Descartes's view, the two things are *complete* substances (soul and body). In Aquinas's view, there are two *incomplete* substances (soul and matter) that jointly compose a complete substance (a human being).

Thus, Aquinas is a Compound Dualist; he is not a Cartesian Substance Dualist. If Stump is correct, then Aquinas is also a *materialist*

---

12. Ibid., 514–15.
13. See Thomas Aquinas, *Summa Theologia* I–II Q.2 A.2; and idem, *In Libros de anima* L.II, 1.1, 215.
14. Aquinas, *Summa Theologia* I, Q.75 A.4.
15. Thomas Aquinas, *Summa Contra Gentiles* II.69.

insofar as human persons are *material* beings. And so it is easy to see why Compound Dualism has appeared attractive to some Christians, for if it succeeds, it provides a view of human nature that is both dualist and materialist. Unfortunately, I think Compound Dualism is an incoherent view of human nature.

THE TROUBLE WITH COMPOUND DUALISM

I believe there are several insurmountable problems confronting Compound Dualism. First, Aquinas's conception of form or soul is that of an incomplete substance, a "configured configurer," as Stump calls it. But the soul is still, for all that, a substance, albeit an incomplete one. Moreover, the soul is an immaterial (incomplete) substance.[16] Therefore, no matter how we slice it, Aquinas's view of persons is still a version of *Substance Dualism*. Now it is *incomplete* substances (not the concrete particular human beings to which they give rise) that are of the material and immaterial kinds. I do not deny that Compound Dualism differs from Descartes's Dualism in interesting and important respects, but even so, we are owed some account of just how an immaterial (incomplete) substance comes to be. Aquinas offers no such account.

Moreover, Compound Dualism suffers from a terminal case of incoherence. Aquinas takes the human soul to be a substantial form. At one point, he concedes that the human soul is a "particular substance."[17] But he also claims that the soul is *not* a substance but, in conjunction with the body, gives rise to one (a human person).[18] Neither Aquinas nor Stump offers a way to reconcile these apparently inconsistent claims. Perhaps what Aquinas really meant to say is that the human soul is not a *complete* substance but, in conjunction with a body, gives rise to one. Perhaps. But then there are still problems. For example, in its disembodied state, the human soul is, with divine assistance, able to engage in intellectual contemplation of God. In-

16. Perhaps according to Aquinas's view incomplete substances are not substances at all, just like plastic wood is not wood and, according to some, artificial intelligence is not intelligence. But given the title of Stump's article and her analysis of Thomistic Dualism, it would seem that for the Stump/Aquinas dualist a human soul *is* a substance, albeit one of an immaterial sort.

17. Aquinas, *Summa Theologia* I, Q.75 A.4.

18. Aquinas, *Summa Contra Gentiles* II.69.

deed, it is able to do many of the sorts of things it used to enable the whole human being to do. It is strange that contemplation of God is going on in the case of a disembodied soul with no one doing the contemplating. It is not that some human person is contemplating God, for there is no human person. There is just a naked soul. And, of course, it is mystery enough how there could even be a naked soul, a substantial form that does not organize any material thing. I do not think this is just a lack of imagination on my part. It is inconsistent with Aquinas's own metaphysics of material substance.

At the end of the day, it strikes me that Compound Dualism is unworkable. However, some see in Aquinas's metaphysics of human nature elements that hold promise for a workable, *non-Cartesian* view of human nature.

A NEW KIND OF DUALISM: EMERGENT DUALISM

William Hasker has argued that human souls or minds are emergent substances and that they relate to human brains as (say) an electromagnetic field relates to its generating source. A magnetic field is an emergent individual; it normally occupies an area larger than its generating magnet and enters into causal commerce with it. So too with human persons, says Hasker. Human persons emerge when biological systems reach the complex level of organization we normally associate with mature human brains in mature human bodies. Hasker contends these immaterial yet spatial emergent substances can bring about changes in the bodies from which they emerge.

The basic idea behind emergentism in the philosophy of mind is that consciousness and mentality do not appear until physical systems reach a sufficiently high level of configurational complexity. Just as liquidity and solidity are features that require matter to be suitably arranged before they are manifested, so too with consciousness and the mental. According to emergentism, therefore, the appearance of mentality is dependent on a physical system of appropriate complexity.

There is another feature of emergentism, namely, that mentality is, in some important sense, irreducible (it is not really something else under a different description; mentality is not, in other words, reducible to neural firings). It is with respect to this that mentality is unlike liquidity and solidity. For the latter are nothing *over and above* organizational/causal features of matter. But the mental is a novel feature of the world, something that in an important sense cannot be reduced to the neurobiological processes that cause it and, furthermore, something that can exert force on the system from which it emerges.

Those key claims are embraced by all emergentists. But there is a more ambitious sort of emergentism defended by Hasker. Hasker's original contribution to the philosophy of mind has been to claim that consciousness cannot be an emergent *property* of the organisms that exhibit it. It cannot be a property because of what he calls the "unity of consciousness argument." Under normal conditions, consciousness presents itself as a unity. My visual experience of the chair in front of me, for example, is whole and of a piece. My conscious experience of the chair is not fragmented and disintegrated. Now the brain is what some philosophers call a *mereological sum* (a collection of parts with various properties standing in very complex relations to one another). In other words, there is no brain over and above the parts that make it up. What Hasker wants us to see is that none of the parts of the brain, or their parts, has a unified conscious experience, even though some of them no doubt play an important causal role in such an experience. You and I, however, under normal circumstances, do enjoy consciousness as a unified experience. Therefore, Hasker wants to know what physical object enjoys the kind of unified conscious experience you and I experience on a regular basis. The standard materialist faces a problem here. For, any of the obvious candidates he or she puts forward as the subject of a unified conscious experience will, Hasker believes, itself be a mereological sum or aggregate of parts. For example, if a materialist puts forward the central nervous system or the brain, then he or she has not really put forward an *individual*, material thing; rather, he or she has put forward a *plurality* or a *collection* of parts to which we have given the singular name "brain" or "central nervous system." In short, a person's awareness of a unified experience cannot consist in the physical parts of a person modeling part of the experience. Hasker claims that what is needed to explain the unity of consciousness is an emergent substance or subject (i.e., in the case of human beings, an immaterial *person*); it is just such an object that can enjoy a unified conscious experience.

Emergent Dualism, therefore, is supposed to make it much easier to account for the unity of consciousness and is to be preferred to its materialist alternatives for this and other reasons. At the same time, Hasker's Emergent Dualism has what he sees as advantages over standard forms of dualism. For example, according to Hasker, the relationship between mind and body is much closer and natural than with the Cartesian view. For consciousness emerges as part of the natural biological development of human brains in human (and other animal) bodies and is, in fact, dependent on the brain for its emergence.

At the same time, Hasker's brand of emergentism is compatible with Christian belief in postmortem survival. For according to Hasker, just as it is possible for God to maintain a magnetic field in existence after the demise of its source of generation, so too with persons. It is possible, thinks Hasker, for God to keep people in existence even after the bodies that generate them cease to exist.

EMERGENT DUALISM CHALLENGED

I find the unity of consciousness argument wholly persuasive. I too believe that standard, *reductive* versions of materialism cannot plausibly account for the unity of consciousness. Even so, I find Hasker's Emergent Dualism less than compelling. First, Hasker chides Cartesian Dualists for viewing the soul as "fundamentally totally different from the body and bear[ing] no necessary relation to it."[19] One would assume that his Emergent Dualism contrasts with this feature of Cartesian Dualism. But does it? Although the emergent soul is causally dependent on the body for its origin, it bears no metaphysically necessary (i.e., essential) relation to the body. After all, Hasker believes the soul can, with God's help, exist in a disembodied state between death (of the body) and resurrection.

Moreover, the mind or soul is a substance according to Hasker's view. What of the body? Is it a substance too? Given that Hasker refers to his view as Emergent *Dualism*, one would think so. But then doesn't the *Dualism* part of Hasker's emergentism consist just in the fact that the soul is "fundamentally totally different from the body"? If so, then in whatever other ways Emergent Dualism differs from Cartesian Dualism, it does not differ from it in terms of committing itself to two distinct kinds of substance, one material and the

---

19. William Hasker, "On Behalf of Emergent Dualism" in *In Search of the Soul: Four Views of the Mind-Body Problem*, ed. Joel B. Green and Stuart L. Palmer (Downer's Grove, IL: InterVarsity, 2005), 75.

other immaterial. Nor does it differ in terms of the soul bearing no essential relation to the body. For, as mentioned, the soul is capable of *disembodied* existence.

Moreover, it is puzzling that Hasker offers as a strength of his theory the claim that Emergent Dualism establishes a *close* and *natural* connection between the soul and the organism. This "close" connection, in fact, is supposed to "prevent the splitting of the person into two disparate entities."[20] There are two problems with this. First, the connection is not *so close* that the one (the soul) is unable to exist without the other (the body), as we have just seen. If the connection is close and natural, we would expect the soul to be causally dependent on the body not only for its *emergence* but also for its *continued existence*, in this life and the next. Second, even according to Hasker's view, the person—or the human being at least—*is* split into two disparate entities. For we still are left with an immaterial (though spatial) soul and a material body. This is not, of course, to deny the important ways in which Emergent Dualism differs from Cartesian Dualism, but it is to point out that it does not differ in the ways we may be led to believe.

THE PROBLEM OF RE-EMBODIED SOULS

There is a real difficulty in the doctrine of resurrection for the Emergent Dualist, one that Hasker mentions on the last page of his book and handles all too quickly. If what is required for the emergence of a soul is a suitably complex configuration of neural circuitry (or its functional equivalent), then shouldn't one expect the resurrection body God creates to generate its *own* soul? Or does God prevent the natural emergence of a soul in the next life in order to "add from the outside" the persisting soul of the individual? If God "adds from the outside" in the next life, is it such a leap to think that God does it here too (a la Cartesianism)? Perhaps we could claim that the resurrection body is the previously deceased but restored body that originally generated the now disembodied soul. Fair enough. But why, then, doesn't that restored body generate *another* soul? Presumably, what God does to the body in restoring it is to restore it to soul-favorable conditions. But if God does that, it is natural to

20. Ibid., 78–79.

think that it will produce another soul and not just be hospitable to the addition of a soul from the outside.

Hasker's response is to suggest that the resurrected body must not, therefore, *first* be created with soul-producing powers and then have the disembodied soul *added*. Rather, "we must imagine the new body created from the very beginning *as the body of this very soul*; the renewed self must be 'in charge' of the resurrection body right from the start."[21] I do not understand this suggestion. Either God creates something like a corpse or a husk and infuses the soul into it, or God creates the functional equivalent of a human body. If God does the former, then the body will not be hospitable to a soul since souls require the functional complexity of a human body. If God does the latter, then we are back to our original problem: Won't the body produce its own soul? Even if we could make sense of Hasker's suggestion, isn't it open to the Cartesian Dualist to say, "If that's how it is with re-embodied souls, is it really such a stretch to suggest that it is also this way with the initial embodiment of a soul?"

MATERIALISM, UNITY OF CONSCIOUSNESS, AND SPATIAL SOULS

Finally, one of the problems for materialists is the phenomenon of the unity of consciousness. I agree with Hasker that this is a serious problem for materialism, but not *all* versions of materialism. It is a problem for *reductive* versions. It is not a problem for those who embrace a Constitution account of human persons. For example, Hasker would have us ask, "When I am aware of a complex conscious state, what *physical entity* is it that is aware of that state?" The materialist, assumes Hasker, can put forward nothing but collections or aggregates—the brain or the central nervous system, for example. But I answer, "Me!" I am the physical entity that is aware of my visual field, and I am not a plurality (nor is my body), even though I am composed of many parts. And, as I will argue in chapter 3, I am a wholly physical thing, sharing with my body all of the matter that constitutes it.

Let me say just a few more things about Emergent Dualism. First, I cannot help but applaud the challenge Emergent Dualism poses

---

21. See William Hasker, *The Emergent Self* (Ithaca: Cornell University Press, 2000), 235. Emphasis in original.

to a mechanistic kind of materialism, the kind of materialism that dominates current debate within the philosophy of mind. Against that target I find the criticisms of Emergent Dualists wholly persuasive. I just happen to believe that emergent *materialism* (not dualism) and constitutionalism are sufficient to solve the problems posed by reductive materialism. Emergent *Dualism* is unnecessary. But second, it must be admitted that Emergent Dualism is a coherent view of the human person, unlike the dualism of Aquinas. And finally, it is compatible with important Christian teaching concerning the afterlife. Nevertheless, I think Emergent Dualism is false, even if it is coherent.

CONCLUSION

Can a Christian coherently be a Substance Dualist, a Compound Dualist, or an emergentist? The answer is quite clearly yes. *Must* a Christian be a dualist of one of these sorts? Here the answer is no. Is biblical teaching consistent with dualism? Again, the answer is yes. Does biblical teaching *require* a dualist anthropology? The answer to this question is no. I want to postpone, however, a discussion of what the Bible says about anthropology until chapter 6. I do this because I would first like to present animalism and the Constitution View. Postponing consideration of the relevant biblical material will permit us to consider the biblical texts with dualism, animalism, and the proposed alternative—the Constitution View—all before us. That will place us in a better position to consider how well the proposed alternative coheres with the biblical witness. In any event, if a dualistic anthropology is rejected, many think that the only alternative to dualism is to claim that we are our bodies. Therefore, it is to a consideration of person-body identity (or animalism) that we now turn.

2

Nothing-But Materialism

I N T H E   L A S T   C H A P T E R   W E looked at reasons and arguments for the claim that we are fundamentally, at least in part, immaterial souls. Such a view was rejected. If dualism is rejected, however, then the most obvious alternative is the view that we are identical with our bodies. I call this "nothing-but" materialism since, according to it, we are nothing but our bodies, mere biological beasts. In academic philosophy, some version or other of nothing-but materialism represents the consensus position. Interestingly, some think it so obvious as to need no argument. Whether we are, in fact, identical with our bodies is anything but obvious. In this chapter I do two things. First, I consider two ways of understanding the claim that human persons are identical with human bodies. I show that according to either interpretation the claim is false. Second, I consider the plain and richly textured fact of consciousness and show that consciousness presents a mystery for materialism of all varieties. But I also urge that this provides no basis for dualism to claim victory over a materialist view of human nature.

PERSON-BODY IDENTITY

Many nothing-but materialists do not provide reasons for their view of human nature. It is simply assumed to be the truth about us given what is nearly a universal rejection of dualism. But if forced to provide reasons for the view that you and I are nothing but our bodies, one common line of argument might be this:

1. Either a human person is identical with his or her body, or a human person is identical with some nonphysical thing.
2. There are no nonphysical things in the natural world with which a human person might plausibly be said to be identical.
3. Therefore, a human person is identical with his or her body.

While this argument has the virtue of being logically valid, a dualist would reject it on account of premise 2. Premise 2, she would say, is false. Along with the materialist, I think premise 2 is true. I do not believe there are any immaterial things in the natural world, such as immaterial souls, with which a human person might be identical. But like the dualist, I reject the conclusion. I do so on account of premise 1. I believe premise 1 presents us with a false dichotomy. In the next chapter I articulate a view that is neither a form of Cartesian Dualism nor a version of person-body identity. Here, however, I consider what it is people mean when they claim that we human persons are nothing but our bodies.

WHAT WE MEAN BY "HUMAN BODY"

The English words *human body* (or *body* for short) can be used to refer to different things in different contexts. Sometimes the word *body* is used to refer to a mass of material stuff. For example, when speaking of a person's body, one may mean the matter or mass of cellular tissues that compose a person's physical organism. Alternatively, one may mean with those same words the physical organism itself. In the first sense, a human body is what is left behind after a natural death (i.e., a corpse). In the second sense, a human body is an organism, a biological animal, which is essentially living, and what is left behind after a natural death is not a body in this sense at all. Rather, what is left behind is a heap of dead cell stuff. Let's consider each as an interpretation of what someone might mean when they claim that human persons are nothing but their bodies or are identical with their bodies.

The Commonsense View: Bodies as Masses of Matter

Gottfried Wilhelm Leibniz first showed with care and precision just what the identity relation amounts to. The upshot of what Leibniz taught is that some object x and some object y are *identical* if whatever is true of the one is true of the other and vice versa (i.e., if x and y share all their properties). Therefore, to show that some thing x is *not* identical with some thing y, all that is required is to find a property that is had by one and lacked by the other. In the case of persons and bodies, if every property had by the one is had by the other, then the English words *person* and *body* are two terms that refer to a single thing, like Superman and Clark Kent refer to the same guy. But if one has a property lacked by the other, or vice versa, then persons and bodies are *not* identical. Are persons and bodies identical? Are there properties had by persons that are lacked by bodies or had by bodies and lacked by persons? I believe there are. For one, bodies, understood here as masses of matter, continue to exist even after persons die. But surely persons do not. I cannot continue to exist after I die since it is not possible that one and the same thing should both continue to exist and die. My *body* can continue to exist after *I* die. Therefore, I cannot be identical with my body.

I find the above argument utterly persuasive. But there is a line of response open to a person-body identity theorist. If I am identical with my body, then the persistence conditions for me are just the persistence conditions for my body. Persistence conditions for things of different kinds tell us what sorts of changes things of those kinds can undergo or suffer without ceasing to exist. For example, persistence conditions for things like bananas are such that bananas can persist through color changes. A banana that is yellow on Monday can survive through changes that render it brown on Friday. It is not that we have two bananas, one yellow and one brown. We have one banana, and it is yellow at one time and brown at another time. Therefore, a defender of person-body identity might say that since my body *can* continue to exist after I die, so can I. Of course, after my death I will lack a property possessed by me before my death, namely, the property "is alive" or "is conscious." But all that follows from this, a defender of person-body identity might say, is that the property "being alive" or "being conscious" is not a property had by me essentially. If a property had by me is had essentially, then I cannot exist without having that property. The claim here is that I—the very thing that is writing this chapter—can exist without having any thoughts or feelings, without being conscious at all. This is analogous to a banana that can exist without being yellow. Being yellow is not an essential property of bananas.

There are several problems, however, with this line of response. First, we have yet to say just what a person *is*. Although it is notoriously difficult to specify necessary and sufficient conditions for something's being a person, it seems highly plausible to suppose that something that lacks a capacity for consciousness for the entire duration of its existence is not an object that was a person at any point of its existence. Although I believe this, a defender of person-body identity might push the objection further. A body after death possesses neither consciousness nor the capacity for it. But it is a thing such that at *some* times during its existence it *did* possess consciousness. So nothing said so far about persons rules out my continuing to exist as a corpse after I die. Of course, the nature of this postmortem existence may be of a very uninteresting kind. It is nothing like the richly textured conscious existence Scripture promises. But so what, a person-body identity theorist might say.

I think we can say more about what a person is and by so doing see what is wrong with the view that we are identical with our bodies (or corpses, after we die). First, it is at the very least a plausible and modest thesis that a person is, minimally, characterized by a capacity for a certain range of intentional states such as belief, desires, etc., since it is at least plausible to suppose that persons are very much like us. I'll want to say a lot more in the next chapter about what a person is, but for now this will do. Among the intentional states for which persons have a capacity are those that are self-referential and first person. If an object is capable of first-person intentional states, then that object is capable of thinking of itself without use of a name, description, or third-person pronoun. This is not especially intuitive, so let me explain.

Typically, I think of myself in a peculiarly first-person way with pronouns such as *I*, *me*, *mine*, and *my*. To illustrate the difference between thinking of oneself from a first-person perspective and from a third-person perspective, consider the following. When Dick Cheney thinks that he is the vice president of the United States, he might represent his thought with "I am the vice president of the United States." This thought is different from the thought he would express by "Cheney is the vice president . . ." or "The former head of Halliburton is the vice president . . ." since Dick Cheney might be mistaken about his being the former head of Halliburton or ignorant of the fact that he is Dick Cheney. (Suppose Dick Cheney is suffering from a severe case of amnesia such that he does not know he is Dick Cheney and is unaware that he is the former head of Halliburton.)

If the capacity for intentional states is a *necessary* (though not sufficient) condition for an object to be a person, then consciousness itself is a necessary condition for something to be a person. For something that lacks all capacity for consciousness will lack the capacity for such states. But dead bodies lack a capacity for consciousness. Therefore, after death, there is no longer a person. Since the body is still there but the person is not, the person cannot be identical with the body.

This argument is not likely to persuade a person-body identity theorist of the sort we are considering. He or she could point out that we are not entitled to the conclusion. All we are entitled to is the conclusion that *after death* a body is not a person. It does not follow, however, that the body is not a person.

As a matter of logic, this is true. But it does follow that *either* a person is not identical with his or her body or after death he or she ceases to be a person. So let us add the following premise to the original argument:

(P) Persons are essentially persons.

If (P) is true, then the thing that is a person is a person for the entire duration of its existence. If that is so, then it is not possible that an object that is a person before death can persist after death and fail to be a person.

Are persons essentially persons? It seems so to me. Indeed, most of us seem to think that other medium-sized physical objects are essentially the kinds of objects they are. For example, my house is essentially an artifact. My house could not have been a dog or a banana. And if a tornado came through town and completely dismantled my house, leaving only a heap of bricks and mortar, then I think most of us uncorrupted by philosophy would say that my house has ceased to exist. What remains is its constituting matter. In the same way, it seems to me that a person is essentially a person such that what sometimes persists after a person's death is its constituting matter or, as we are presently understanding the term, its *body*.

Suppose, for the sake of argument, that persons are *not* essentially persons and that bodies are merely masses of matter. Such a view has highly counterintuitive implications. First, it requires, for example, that "George W. Bush" names a mass of cell stuff. Imagine that the mass of cell stuff that we refer to with the name of "George W. Bush" never was a person, because it never was conscious. If the mass of cell stuff never was a person, then it likely never would be referred to with the name "George W. Bush." Even so, George W. Bush, the very thing that actually exists and is a person, would still exist; it just would not be a person. So in our imagined scenario, "George W. Bush" names a mass of cell stuff, even though that mass of cell stuff is not a person. We could even imagine that the mass of cell stuff we refer to with the name "George W. Bush" never composed an organism. Still, if "George W. Bush" names a collection of atoms, then George W. Bush would still exist in this scenario.

Contrary to what we have been imagining, it seems to me much more plausible to suppose that "George W. Bush" names a *person* and not the mass of cell stuff that constitutes him. To anticipate the discussion in the next chapter, names usually refer to constituted objects, not the objects that constitute them.

In the end, I simply cannot take seriously the suggestion that I could have existed without ever having been a person. I can imagine existing and not ever having taught at Calvin College. I can imagine existing and being very much different from what I am (perhaps being 6'6" tall, being a star basketball player, or being a trial lawyer). But I simply cannot imagine what it would mean for me, this very individual, to exist without ever having been a person.

The consequences of assuming that persons are *not* essentially persons casts, in my mind, overwhelming doubt on that claim. If the implications of the view do not present overwhelming obstacles for person-body identity theorists, there is really not much else I can say. The best I can do is appeal to their intuitions, to ask if they think it really is possible that they—the sentient, thinking, feeling, rational, relational creatures they are—could exist without being a person, without being a sentient, thinking, feeling, rational, and relational creature.[1]

1. It is important to point out here that I have been speaking in terms of a *capacity* for intentional states and consciousness. I do this quite intentionally so as not to exclude from the class of persons comatose and other unconscious patients who may not *exercise* those capacities at certain times.

Since I think persons are essentially persons, I think my original objection establishes that persons are *not* identical with bodies, bodies being construed as masses of cell stuff. The argument presented for the nonidentity of persons and bodies rests, of course, on a premise that appeals to our intuitions. It rests on the claim that persons are essentially persons. That seems to me a plausible claim and to be in keeping with how we think about other kinds of physical objects, like houses, statues, and cats. Of course, if one does not believe that persons are essentially persons, I can only try to highlight the unattractiveness of denying that claim.

There are other problems, however, with treating bodies merely as masses of matter and claiming that we are identical with our bodies. One problem is that the mass of matter that composes me now is different from the mass of matter that composed me twenty years ago and even different from the mass of matter that composed me before I bumped into the wall and shaved off a few dead skin cells that lay near my surface. According to the current construal of "body," either I am identical with lots of different masses of matter, or the person who existed before the bump into the wall is not, strictly speaking, the same person as the person who exists after the bump. In other words, if I existed before the bump, and there is a person around after the bump, that person is not me. Surely one thing—me—cannot be identical with many different things. Therefore, I am not identical with lots of different masses. And it is difficult to believe that the person who exists after the bump into the wall is not me. It seems that I was around before and after the bump. But if bodies are masses of matter, and I am identical with a mass of matter, then as soon as the mass of matter I am ceases to exist (after the bump), there will be a different mass of matter and so a different person. But this seems to strain our credulity. So if I am around before and after the bump into the wall, then I am not identical with my body. I am not identical with my body because my body, according to the present view, is a mass of cell stuff, and the mass of cell stuff that exists after the bump into the wall is not the same as the mass that existed before the bump.

So, there are many reasons for denying that we human persons are identical with our bodies, bodies being construed as masses of matter. This brings us to a more nuanced way of understanding the claim that persons are identical with bodies.

The Animalist View

I am seated in a chair in my dining room as I write this sentence. There is a human organism sitting in a chair in my dining room. According to animalism, I and the human organism are one and the same thing. That human organism *is* me. I am a human animal. Since dualism has such a hold on us Christians, we are likely to think it obviously false that we are animals. But in the larger community, many find it just as obvious that we *are* human animals. It is not difficult to see why either, especially given the underlying metaphysical reductionism that permeates popular culture. We can express the view this way. If whatever is is physical, then what else might we be if not human animals? We are not dogs, computers, or gods. Contrary to the thesis entertained in the last section, we are not masses of matter. We are human beings, and a human being is, by definition, a kind of animal, a member of the species *Homo sapiens*. To put it baldly, according to animalism, we are the highly complex organisms that are our bodies.

Before we look at some of the reasons for believing that we are animals, consider first what an animal is. For starters, animals are biological organisms along with other biological organisms like plants and bacteria. Now that is true so far as it goes, but when we ask, What is an animal? we want to know what it takes for something to count as an animal. What are the necessary and sufficient conditions for something's being an animal? That is a question that deserves a book-length treatment itself. Since I cannot offer such a treatment here, let me suggest the following.

First, an animal is an individual thing or substance. It is not a property (like being green) or a state (like suspension) or a collection or aggregate (like a heap of atoms or cellular tissues). Organisms also have or undergo a process called life; they are *living* things. I say more about this in chapter 3. But let it suffice to say here that lives are self-maintaining processes or events. Finally, organisms have parts, lots of them, and they can be composed of different parts at different times. Indeed, if an organism is to persist through time, if it is to remain alive, it has to be made of different parts at different times.

Nothing said so far helps us distinguish human from nonhuman animals. For dogs and cats are animals too. However, human animals, in contrast to nonhuman animals (at least as far as we know), *think.* One contemporary philosopher[2] uses the property of thinking to construct an argument for animalism. (Remember Descartes used the same property to motivate an argument for dualism.)

1. There is a human animal sitting in my chair.
2. The human animal sitting in my chair is thinking.
3. I am the thinking being sitting in my chair.
4. The one and only thinking thing sitting in my chair is me.
5. Therefore, I am that thinking animal.

Of course, I am not unique. If I am an animal, then you are too. This is a simple argument, and most (if not all) animalists would endorse it. What is to be said on behalf of the premises that make up the argument? Well, I think the animalist endorses the premises by considering how and on what basis the premises might be denied. In essence, an animalist thinks the reasons given for the denials of the premises are less plausible than the premises themselves. So until he or she hears a good reason to deny one or more of the premises, he or she feels entitled to them.

OBJECTIONS TO ANIMALISM

It will come as no surprise that I find at least one of the premises to this argument false. I agree that there is a human animal sitting in my chair, and so I see no need to dispute the first premise. But I do not believe that the human animal sitting in my chair is thinking. I think the human animal sitting in my chair is doing (or at least its brain is doing) lots of things that are essential to thinking. But it is *me* that is thinking and not it. Consider: Is it my eyes that see, or do I see in virtue of my eyes? Is it my hand that votes in a departmental meeting, or do I vote in virtue of doing something with my hand? I think it is pretty obvious that my eyes do not see but that I see in virtue of my eyes. It is not my hand that votes but I that vote in virtue of motioning with my hand. Or consider this: Is it my leg that is held morally responsible for kicking the dog, or am I held morally responsible for kicking the dog? You get the point. The body, and more particularly the brain, undergoes lots of interesting processes that are integral to thinking. But I think it is as wrong to attribute

2. Eric Olson is the philosopher, and he uses the argument that follows in a book he is working on for his belief that he is a thinking animal.

thinking to the body or the brain as it is to attribute seeing to the eyes or voting to the hand. It is *persons* that think, not the animals that constitute them.

Am I saying then that human persons are not animals? Emphatically yes. We are not animals, at least not in the sense of being *identical with* animals. But is there a sense in which human persons *are* animals? Well, yes, there is a sense in which it is true to say that we are animals. Obviously, this sense must be different from the sense in which we are identical with animals. The sense in which we are animals is the sense in which it is correct to say that we are *wholly constituted* by animals; every material part of me is a part of the animal that constitutes me, and no parts of me are immaterial. I say more about constitution in the next chapter. But let me say here that in the ordinary business of life we do not distinguish between the "is" or "are" of constitution and the "is" or "are" of identity. Generally speaking, we have no need to. But it is, nevertheless, an important metaphysical distinction. It is akin to the distinction between having a cold and having the flu. In the ordinary business of life, we do not distinguish between having the flu and having a cold. There is really no need to. But, of course, the distinction is important for purposes of medical treatment. For now, let me say more about why I believe we are not identical with our bodies by considering the implications of the view.

Implausible Implications of Animalism

If animalism is true, then you have the same persistence conditions as an animal. Consider the following fanciful scenario. Suppose some crazed surgeon took all of your brain out except for your brain stem. Your brain stem is the command center for all the biological processes necessary for biological life such as respiration, digestion, the circulation of blood, the regulation of metabolism, and so on. If animalism is true, then you last as long as your biological life lasts. Therefore, if animalism is true, since your body can persist without a cerebral cortex, so can you. In the imagined scenario, you would be reduced, quite literally, to a respiring, slobbering, excreting, metabolizing human animal. That is to say, the empty-headed entity respiring, metabolizing, excreting, and circulating blood is you. Granted, the empty-headed beast is not conscious and does not even possess the capacity for conscious experience (having lost its cerebral cortex, which appears to be a causal requirement for human consciousness). Nevertheless, that beast is you.

I said earlier that I believe that anything that is a person is essentially a person. In other words, a person cannot exist without being a person, just as a particular dog (Lassie, say) cannot exist and fail to be a dog. Since a capacity for consciousness is necessary (but not sufficient) for something's being a person, the biological beast that exists without a cerebral cortex is not a person and so not you, for you are surely a person if anything is.

In the end, I see no good reason to believe that persons are not essentially persons. Since animalism entails that things that are persons are not persons essentially, I find the view unbelievable. Persons are not identical with their animal bodies.

THE MYSTERY OF CONSCIOUSNESS AND MATERIALISM

In the last chapter we saw how William Hasker uses the unity of consciousness experience against reductionistic or nothing-but materialism. Hasker's point, it will be recalled, is that the unity of consciousness requires a subject who enjoys the unified experience. The problem is that the reductionist can provide no individual as the subject of the unified conscious experience. And this is so, Hasker maintains, because the most plausible candidates the reductionist might put forward as the subject (e.g., the brain, the central nervous system, or the organism itself) are *aggregates* or collections of parts. If the brain, for example, is nothing over and above the parts that make it up, then we are without a subject to account for the unity of conscious experience.

While some animalists would no doubt agree with Hasker about brains and central nervous systems (i.e., that there aren't any such things over and above the smallest parts that make them up), they would, I think, argue that things are not so with respect to organisms. Organisms or animals are things over and above the smallest things that compose them. And it is the organism itself, the animalist might say, that enjoys a unified conscious experience. My aim here is not to adjudicate between Hasker and the animalist concerning the unity of consciousness. My aim is to look at consciousness and the mental and to ask this question: Does the sheer fact of consciousness tip the scales in favor of dualism over a materialist view of persons?

It must be frankly admitted that consciousness is a stumbling block for materialists. Period. Here is how one materialist, Colin McGinn, puts it:

> How is it possible for conscious states to depend upon brain states? How can technicolour phenomenology arise from soggy grey matter? Somehow we feel the water of the brain is turned into the wine of consciousness, but we draw a total blank on the nature of this conversion.[3]

Solving the mystery of consciousness in materialist terms, however, has simply proven intractable for materialists. Why does consciousness seem to escape the materialist net, no matter how wide that net is cast? Is it because no naturalistic link exists between neurophysiological goings-on in the brain and technicolor phenomenology? Is there a solution to the mystery that characterizes the relationship between the mental and the physical?

McGinn would have us believe that there is good news and bad news. The good news is that there is a *natural* property that accounts for the psychophysical link:

> Resolutely shunning the supernatural, I think it is undeniable that it must be in virtue of *some* natural property of the brain that organisms are conscious. There just *has* to be some explanation for how brains subserve minds.[4]

Now the bad news. Our cognitive constitution is such that the psychophysical connection, the natural property of the brain in virtue of which consciousness arises, will remain ever beyond our cognitive grasp. Consciousness is and forever will be a mystery to us.

I believe that there is both good and bad in this assessment of the mystery of consciousness. First, I think it is correct that it is in virtue of some natural property of brains that organisms are conscious and that therefore there must be a naturalistic explanation for how brains subserve minds. We must be careful here, however, because McGinn makes such assertions on the basis of "resolutely shunning the super-

---

3. Colin McGinn, "Can We Solve the Mind-Body Problem?" in *The Problem of Consciousness: Essays toward a Resolution*, 2nd ed. (Cambridge, MA: Blackwell, 1994), 1–2.
4. Ibid., 6.

natural." And I think what McGinn means by "resolutely shunning the supernatural" is to rule out, *a priori*, the existence of God, the soul, or anything supernatural or immaterial. To put it another way, McGinn is a *metaphysical* naturalist (a naturalist about *everything*: The natural world is all there is, and so it is exhaustive of reality). But one need not embrace that thoroughly secular claim in order to believe that it is in virtue of some natural property of brains that organisms are conscious.

For example, I am a theist, a supernaturalist, you might say. As such, I believe in God the Father almighty, maker of heaven and earth. And since I believe in the God of Christian Scripture, I believe neither that the natural world is all there is nor that the natural world is "causally closed." I believe, in other words, that God can intervene in the natural world, that God has done so, and that God continues to do so. Nevertheless, I believe that, *for the most part*, God does not *directly* intervene in the natural world. Since the natural world has yielded in so many ways to scientific explanation over the past several hundred years, it seems only plausible to believe that God created the world—the *natural* world—with its own integrity, such that it operates according to regularities that can be grasped and understood not only by those who acknowledge its author but also by those who do not and whose explanations, though accurate, do not appeal to the author of nature. Anyone who would deny that this is so must also deny that genuine contributions to our understanding of the natural world have been made by atheist and agnostic scientists. The situation, in other words, is similar to the situation with morality. God set up the moral universe with integrity, such that it is graspable and understandable not only by those who acknowledge its author but also by those who do not and whose moral theories and explanations, though often revelatory of reality, do not appeal to the author of morality. Anyone who would deny that this is so must also deny that atheists and agnostics can lead moral lives and offer genuine insight into the nature of morality.[5]

Since God created the natural world and all that it contains with its own integrity, it is also reasonable to believe that consciousness itself—a feature encountered in the natural world—has a *natural*

---

5. I was pleased to discover that Donald MacKay makes nearly the same point I make here and in the next paragraph in his *Science, Chance, and Providence* (New York: Oxford University Press, 1978).

explanation. In other words, we can accept McGinn's assertion that it is in virtue of a *natural* property of the brain that organisms are conscious without accepting his metaphysical naturalism.

It may be helpful here to distinguish *metaphysical* naturalism from both *methodological* naturalism and what we might call *chastened* naturalism. Metaphysical naturalism, as we have seen, amounts to the claim that the natural world is all there is and is exhaustive of reality. Methodological naturalism, on the other hand, amounts to a presupposition about the practice of science. It says that scientific explanations must exclude reference to supernatural or immaterial entities. Since science is in the business of discovering natural causes, this should not surprise us. Methodological naturalism is compatible with a robust Christian theism insofar as it does not rule out explanations that appeal to God. It simply would not count such explanations as *scientific* explanations. Finally, chastened naturalism recognizes the enormous contribution science has made to our understanding of the natural world and sees the natural world as possessing its own integrity and exemplifying regularities that can be understood without reference to immaterial or supernatural entities. What makes it *chastened* naturalism is its refusal to go "metaphysical" and to claim that the natural world is all there is and therefore that the sciences are the *only* sources of genuine knowledge. Chastened naturalism is compatible with the existence of religious experience and divine revelation. Such experience and revelation provide for religious *knowledge*, which is genuine knowledge even if not visible to the practice of science and by definition not *scientific* knowledge. Therefore, granting that it is in virtue of some *natural* property of brains that organisms are conscious does not require us to sacrifice our Christian commitments.

Let us now consider what I find problematic about McGinn's argument. The conclusion to McGinn's argument is essentially this: We are constitutionally ill suited for understanding the psychophysical link between mind and body. We are not just waiting for some Einstein-like genius to come along and present us with the solution. This conclusion partly depends on the claim that we simply cannot conceive of a perceptible property of the brain, or a property legitimately inferred from a perceptible property of the brain, that would make the mind-body relation intelligible.[6]

6. McGinn, "Can We Solve the Mind-Body Problem?" 11.

The problem here is that McGinn is simply not warranted in moving from our present conceptual limitations to the claim that these limitations are *constitutional.* One can imagine a primitive inferring from his failure to conceive how a human artifact could become and sustain being airborne for long stretches of time that this inability is constitutional; he is not merely waiting for some genius to come along and expand his conceptual horizons. Well, as a matter of fact, a genius of sorts *did* come along and has rendered imaginable what once was unimaginable. Likewise, the problem with discovering the psychophysical link between brains and consciousness may lie not in human constitution but rather in our present conceptual limitations.

I am not claiming that consciousness is not at present a baffling mystery. It is. Consciousness, in all its variegated reality, has not yet yielded itself to natural explanation. My point is simply that this may say more about our powers of imagination than about the in-principle impossibility of discovering its explanation.

Finally, it is strange that McGinn considers his "mysterianism" a solution, albeit a nonconstructive solution, to the problem of consciousness. His claim is that the relationship between mind and body "has a full and non-mysterious explanation in a certain science, but that this science is inaccessible to us as a matter of principle."[7] This seems a hard pill to swallow for a naturalist of any stripe insofar as it would seem to entail that the properties of mind cannot in fact be explained in natural terms. Indeed, McGinn acknowledges as much.[8] But then I think it is fair to conclude that McGinn's "mysterianism" is inadequate as a *solution* to the problem of consciousness.

The Mystery of Consciousness: Equal Opportunity Employer

So what is the solution to the problem of consciousness? I must say quite frankly that I haven't much to offer in the way of a solution. Like McGinn and Leibniz before him, I think consciousness continues to prove itself insoluble for naturalists. It remains, as I have suggested, a mystery. But unlike McGinn, I cannot see that there is much to his proposed "solution" to the mystery. If I am right, that consciousness

7. Ibid., 17.
8. Ibid., 23.

is mysterious in just the way McGinn and Leibniz say it is, and it is also the case that materialists in general, and McGinn in particular, have failed to demystify it, then shouldn't this drive us ineluctably back to Substance Dualism? I think not. What I want to do now is to say why this is so; to say why the fact of consciousness, though profoundly puzzling to naturalists, ought not to be viewed by dualists as grounds for celebrating victory in the mind-body debate.

It is true that dualists sometimes seem to treat materialism's inability to fit consciousness comfortably into their naturalism as somehow contributing to the likelihood of dualism.[9] The argument would seem to go something like this:

1. Materialism or dualism is true.
2. We human beings are conscious creatures.
3. It is a mystery how it is that we human beings are conscious creatures if materialism is true.
4. Therefore, the fact that we human beings are conscious creatures is a good reason for believing dualism is true.

It is not too difficult to see the problems with this line of argument.[10] First, we are not the only kind of creatures that are conscious. Dogs, cats, and other kinds of creatures also seem to enjoy a range of conscious experience. Therefore, if dualism is true about us, then it seems equally plausible to believe that it is true about those other kinds of creatures too. At least some dualists seem unwilling to admit this.

Moreover, suppose we know about John that he is either a full-time auto mechanic or a full-time janitor. Suppose we also know that John attends philosophy colloquia at Calvin College every Tuesday afternoon. The fact that it is difficult to see how it could be that John attends philosophy colloquia at Calvin every Tuesday afternoon *if* John is an auto mechanic is no good reason to believe he is

9. John Foster seems to take this line in "A Defense of Dualism," in *The Case for Dualism*, ed. John R. Smythies and John Beloff (Charlottesville: University Press of Virginia, 1989), 1–23. See especially p. 9, where Foster contends that the fact that consciousness is resistant to a materialist account seems at the very least to oblige us to accept dualism with respect to beliefs, thoughts, and the like.

10. Peter van Inwagen criticizes the same line of argument in *Metaphysics* (Ithaca: Cornell University Press, 1990), especially pp. 160–63; and also in "Dualism and Materialism: Athens and Jerusalem?" *Faith and Philosophy* 12 (1995): 475–88.

a janitor. In other words, it needs to be shown how John's attending philosophy colloquia makes it more likely that he is a janitor than an auto mechanic.

Could it be argued, however, that it is much easier to see how we human beings are conscious if dualism is true than if we are wholly physical beings (i.e., if some version of materialism is true)? This at least is a more promising form of argument. But again, I do not find it ultimately persuasive. Here is why. Is it really any easier to see how an immaterial soul could be conscious than to see how a material being could be? It does not seem so. If anything, it may seem harder, owing simply to the fact that it is difficult to imagine an immaterial soul. In fact, Peter van Inwagen has argued for the claim that since we know quite a lot about physical objects, the mystery of consciousness is glaring.[11] There is, he believes, a corresponding *ignorance* about nonphysical objects that has had the tendency to conceal the mystery for dualists. But the fact of the matter really is this: Consciousness is a mystery for all of us. It is no less a mystery for dualists than for materialists. Therefore, the fact that consciousness is profoundly baffling to materialists does not threaten in the least a materialist metaphysics of human persons.

I have often heard it said that since God is a person and is immaterial, and since we are persons created in God's image, then it simply follows that we are immaterial, being persons ourselves. I want to postpone a discussion on what it means to be created in the image of God,[12] but it is worth pointing out here that, although we are surely persons, we are also, equally surely, *embodied* persons, quite unlike God the Father in that regard. But more importantly, God's experience or awareness of the natural world, being unmediated by a body, must be quite different from human consciousness or awareness of the natural world, which is mediated by a body. Recall that human awareness of the natural world is marked by that "technicolor phenomenology" that McGinn speaks about. God's awareness, it is plausible to assume, lacks that kind of phenomenology. Therefore, if we are immaterial souls, I simply cannot see how that fact itself goes any distance toward demystifying the very fact of human consciousness. Again, consciousness is admittedly a mystery for materialists, but it is no less (and perhaps even more so) a mystery for dualists.

11. Van Inwagen, *Metaphysics*, 160–63.
12. Chapter 3 says more about this.

CONCLUSION

The obvious alternative to Cartesian Dualism is the view that we are our bodies. Yet I have argued that this is false. We are not our bodies. Consciousness, I have argued, is a deeply mysterious phenomenon that materialists have failed to explain adequately. Nevertheless, I have argued that consciousness is no less a mystery for dualists, and therefore the fact of consciousness provides no reason for preferring dualism over materialism. The next chapter offers an alternative view of human nature according to which we human persons are neither immaterial souls nor material bodies. It argues, on the contrary, that we are wholly physical creatures constituted by our bodies without being identical with them.

3

The Constitution View

So far we have looked at two views of human nature, dualism and animalism. As we have seen, according to Substance Dualism, a person is an immaterial substance, a soul. According to Compound Dualism, a person is at least partially composed of an immaterial soul, even if he or she is not, strictly speaking, identical with an immaterial soul. According to animalism, a person is identical with a human animal. What many find surprising about my view is that while I do not identify myself with an immaterial soul or a compound of soul and body, neither do I believe I am identical with the physical object that is my biological body. But how can that be? If I am not an immaterial soul or a compound of soul and body, how could I possibly be a physical object if I am not the physical object that is my body? This chapter attempts to explain this. What I offer here is a middle way, an alternative to dualism, on the one hand, and animalism, on the other.

CONSTITUTION, IDENTITY, AND ARTIFACTS

The view of human persons defended in this chapter is the Constitution View (CV). According to CV, we human persons are *constituted by* our bodies without being identical with the bodies that constitute us. This claim is not an *ad hoc* claim. Many medium-sized physical objects stand in constitution relations. For example, statues are often constituted by pieces of marble, copper, or bronze, but statues are not identical with the pieces of marble, copper, or bronze that constitute them. Likewise, dollar bills, diplomas, and dust jackets are often constituted by pieces of paper, but none of those things is identical with the piece of paper that constitutes it. Why? Because of the test employed in chapter 2 for determining whether a thing x is identical with a thing y. Are there any properties that the one has but the other lacks? If so, then x and y are not identical. Are there any changes that x could undergo without ceasing to exist but which y could not undergo without ceasing to exist or vice versa? If so, then x and y are numerically distinct things. Even if x and y *possibly* differ, then x and y are not identical.

As discussed in chapter 1, outside philosophy we use the term *identical* or the phrase *the same as* in a loose and nontechnical sense. We might say, for example, that your car is "the same as" mine or that we have "identical" shirts. What we mean is that our cars or shirts are phenomenologically indistinguishable. But philosophers use the term *identical* or the phrase *the same as* strictly in terms of number, the number one. With respect to number, of course, you and I do not have *the same* book or shirt. You have one, and I have one, and one plus one makes two.

Consider the case of a particular copper statue. Is the piece of copper numerically the same as the statue? I think not. It is possible for the piece of copper to survive changes that would put an end to the existence of the statue. For example, extreme heat or repeated blows with a sledge hammer might destroy the statue but not the copper. Why not the copper? Because we can imagine the piece of copper surviving being hammered flat but not the statue. A single thing cannot both survive and fail to survive the same changes. Therefore, if the piece of copper can survive changes that would destroy the statue, then the piece of copper is not identical with the statue. Similar distinctions apply to dollar bills, tables, physical organisms of various kinds, and the things that constitute them.

According to a metaphysics of constitution, therefore, two material objects stand in constitution relations to one another only if the objects are (1) spatially coincident (wholly occupy the same space) and (2) belong to different kinds. To say that two material objects are spatially coincident is a fancy way of saying that the objects share the same matter. In other words, every atom that composes the one composes the other. The statue and the piece of copper share the same matter and therefore are spatially coincident. (This is why defenders of CV say that constitution is as close as one can get to identity *without* identity. Since two objects that stand in constitution relations share all the same matter, one cannot pull them apart.) But pieces of copper and statues are, obviously, objects of different kinds. Indeed, as we have seen, an object of the one kind can survive changes that would terminate the existence of an object of the other kind.[1]

That is the general shape of the constitution relation. Although Aristotle did not hold a Constitution View of medium-sized physical objects, I would suggest that CV bears certain similarities to Aristotle's metaphysics of material substance. I say this to highlight the fact that CV did not drop down from on high in the twenty-first century with no historical antecedents. Elements of the view are, I believe, in Aristotle's view, as well as in John Locke's, for example.

PERSONS, BODIES, AND CONSTITUTION

Let's apply CV specifically to human persons. According to a constitution account, human persons are constituted by bodies but are not identical with the bodies that constitute them. Why say so? First, consider what it is in virtue of which an object is a *person* and what it is in virtue of which an object is a *body*. Though it is difficult to state conditions that all and only persons satisfy, we can say with some confidence that persons (human or otherwise) are, minimally, beings with a capacity for intentional states (e.g., believing, desiring, intending, etc.). Intentional states are *about* things or are *directed at* things. For example, we have beliefs *about* the weather or math or our spouse. Our desires are *directed toward* a new car, a promotion, or growing in devotion to Jesus. By contrast, water flowing through a radiator or the electrical currents flowing through a circuit are not *about* anything.

I say persons are "minimally" beings with the capacity for intentional states because, of course, there are things that satisfy the

---

1. For those who prefer bells and whistles, here is a characterization of the relationship using logical notation: x constitutes y only if: (1) x and y wholly occupy the same space, and (2) there are different sortal properties F and G and an environment E such that (1) (Fx and x is in E) and (Gy and y is in E) and (2) ($\forall$z) [(Fz and z is in E) $\supset$ ($\exists$w) (Gw and w is in E) and (w $\neq$ z)].

condition that it is plausible to believe are *not* persons (e.g., dogs). Dogs too have desires and even, I would suggest, simple beliefs, such as *there is food over there.* My point is this: If something (a rock or a washing machine, for example) does not so much as have a capacity for intentional states, it seems obvious that the thing is not a candidate for personhood. Therefore, if a being lacks a capacity for intentional states, then that being, whatever it is, is not a person.

Moreover, persons are also the only sort of thing that has what Lynne Baker calls a *first-person perspective.*[2] A first-person perspective is more than just a perspective on the world or a locus of consciousness, for lots of nonpersonal creatures (like dogs) have that. A first-person perspective is the capacity to think of oneself as *oneself* without the need of a description or third-person pronoun. For example, I can think of myself as myself without thinking of myself as Kevin Corcoran, without thinking of myself as the father of Shannon and Rowan Corcoran, or without thinking of myself as the sole Irishman in the Calvin philosophy department. When I wonder, for example, whether I will live long enough to see my children graduate from college, I am thinking of myself from the first-person perspective.[3] Finally, according to my view, not only are human persons *essentially*[4] bodily beings, insofar as they are now constituted by biological bodies,[5] but human persons are *essentially*

2. See Lynne Baker, *Persons and Bodies* (New York: Cambridge University Press, 2000), especially chap. 3.

3. It is this feature of personhood that all nonhuman animals seem to lack and that disqualifies them from personhood.

4. When I use the term *essential* and its cognates, I have a special meaning in mind. For starters, we need to distinguish between substance and properties. Think of substances as individual things and properties as ways those things can be or fail to be. For example, being six feet tall, being green, and weighing two hundred pounds are examples of properties. Now some things have those properties, and some do not. Some properties are had *contingently* by the things that have them, and others are had *essentially.* If a substance has a property essentially, then that substance cannot exist and fail to have that property. If a substance has a property contingently, then that substance can exist without having that property. For example, you may have the property of weighing two hundred pounds. But surely you could exist without weighing two hundred pounds. You may either gain or lose that property without ceasing to exist. But take a particular dog, Lassie, for example. Lassie has the property of being a canine. Lassie could not exist without being a canine. So, Lassie is essentially a canine. If Lassie should cease to be a canine, Lassie would cease to exist.

5. Here I reveal my commitment to the claim that material objects are *essentially* material. Take my son's baseball mitt, for example. I do not believe that that very

constituted by the biological bodies that do in fact constitute them. Therefore, if my body should ever cease to exist, I would cease to exist.[6] Now, let's get a little clearer on what I mean by a "biological body." I mean, quite simply, a physical *organism*. And according to a constitution account of physical organisms, they are constituted objects, being constituted by masses of cellular tissues. Moreover, by "physical organism" I mean a living animal, and by "living" I have in mind an individual biological process of a special sort, a sort that is remarkably stable, well individuated, self-directing, self-maintaining, and homeodynamic.[7]

Now one reason for denying that human persons are identical with the physical organisms that constitute them is that the kinds "person" and "physical organism" have different *identity* conditions. For example, there is nothing in the criterion of identity for an organism that involves having intentional states. Therefore, a conceptual impossibility is not involved in thinking about the physical organism that is my body existing while completely lacking a capacity for intentional states. If what I said above is true, however, then there is such an impossibility involved in the idea of *my* existing while lacking all capacity for intentional states, for I am a person. This is why I believe that, while I am constituted by my body, I am not, strictly speaking, identical with it. Indeed, I believe that my body came into existence *before* I did, and it is conceivable that my body will outlive me. I am therefore not my body, since I cannot possibly have come into existence before I did, nor can I conceivably outlive myself.

---

mitt can exist and fail to be a material object. This plausible claim is, for all its plausibility, not uncontroversial. Some philosophers think that some material objects are merely *contingently* material. Someone who believes that my son's baseball mitt is only contingently material believes that though it in fact is material it could exist without being material. I do not believe that.

6. It should be pointed out that the Constitution View of persons is a metaphysical view of the relationship between a human person and his or her body. It is not a theory of the mind and the relationship between mental events (e.g., being in pain, etc.) and physical events in the brain (e.g., the firing of neurons). As I understand the view, it is neutral with respect to so-called reductive and nonreductive theories of mind.

7. For a more detailed account of life and why a wave, flame, or tornado does not count as an instance of life, see Peter van Inwagen, *Material Beings* (Ithaca: Cornell University Press, 1990), 81–97.

THE PERSISTENCE OF PERSONS AND BODIES

Persistence conditions tell us the sorts of changes a thing can undergo without ceasing to exist. In an earlier chapter we considered a thing like a banana, which might be yellow on Monday and can survive changes such as those that result in a brown banana on Friday. But a thing like a banana cannot survive changes such as those involved in making banana bread. In other words, things like bananas can survive *color* changes, but they cannot survive *smashings* and *mixings*. The question to consider now is this: What are the persistence conditions for persons and bodies according to a constitution account of them? What sorts of changes can a person or body survive without ceasing to exist?

It is often thought that continuity through time and space is, if not sufficient, at least necessary for the persistence of bodies.[8] If we cannot, as it were, trace an unbroken line from one time and place to some other time and place without ever losing the object we are tracking, then the object has not persisted from the one time and place to the other time and place. However, there are good reasons for claiming that spatiotemporal continuity is neither necessary nor sufficient for the survival of physical organisms. Let's begin by considering the insufficiency of spatiotemporal continuity for the survival of physical organisms by examining the following far-fetched example. It seems possible that an evil genius could annihilate a body during a certain interval of time and that God could replace it with a newly created molecular duplicate during precisely the same interval and in precisely the same place as that once occupied by the original body at the time of its annihilation. The picture is that of the gradual top down annihilation of one body and the replacement of it with a numerically distinct duplicate, the replacement body exactly filling the human body-shaped receptacle created by the annihilated body. In

8. Philosophers often distinguish between necessary and sufficient conditions. For example, a necessary condition for something to be a bicycle is that it has wheels and is used for human transportation. This isn't enough, however, for an object to be a bicycle. What is both necessary and *sufficient* for something to be a bicycle is that it has only two wheels and is propelled manually, by pedaling, for example. On the other hand, it is sufficient for someone's being my uncle that the person be identical with John Corcoran. But being identical with John Corcoran is not *necessary* for someone to be my uncle, for I have lots of uncles in addition to John Corcoran. The claim here is that continuity through space and time is necessary if not sufficient for the persistence of things like human bodies.

other words, the same interval of time would mark the *end* of one body's existence and the *beginning* of a duplicate's existence, while the spatial region originally filled by the annihilated body would come to be wholly filled by a body numerically distinct from it. The possibility of a *seamless* replacement of one body with another seems to suggest that continuity through space and time is not enough for the persistence of bodies.[9] Again, it is not enough because the example appears to present us with a case in which there *is* spatiotemporal continuity *without* persistence.

What is important to keep in mind is not how wildly unlikely it would be for such a thing to happen but whether it is a logical possibility. It is the mere *possibility* that illustrates the insufficiency of spatiotemporal continuity as a guarantee for the persistence of a human body. What is more interesting is the fact that there is some reason to believe that spatiotemporal continuity is not even *necessary* for the persistence of bodies. Reflection on such thought experiments as those graphically portrayed on *Star Trek* suggest as much. Occupants of the transporter seem to disappear at one time and from one place only to reemerge at another time and in another place. One interpretation of what happens to those who enter the transporter is that they are able to skip over intervening times and spaces en route to their future destination. What imaginative scenarios like this have suggested to some philosophers is that spatiotemporal continuity is normally merely a *consequence* of persistence and not its ground.[10] In other words, there must be something else that secures persistence. It has been thought that a good candidate for what grounds cases of persistence is some kind of causation. If the cupcake before me has *persisted into* the present, then it seems that its existence in the immediate past must be *causally* relevant to its existence now. So too with human bodies. It seems that if a human body sitting before me at 9:00 a.m. is not *causally* connected with one that was sitting before me at 8:59 a.m., then it is plausible to think that the human body before me at 9:00 a.m. is not a *continuation* of the body that was before me at 8:59 a.m. but is rather a numerically distinct re-

9. The idea of "smooth" replicas or "immaculate" replacements can be credited either to Sydney Shoemaker, "Identity, Properties, and Causality," in *Identity, Cause, and Mind* (Cambridge: Cambridge University Press, 1984), 234–60; or David Armstrong, "Identity through Time," in *Time and Cause*, ed. Peter van Inwagen (Dordrecht: D. Reidel, 1980), 67–78.

10. See, for example, Armstrong, "Identity through Time," 76.

placement, even if there is spatiotemporal continuity between the 9:00 a.m. body and the 8:59 a.m. body and even if the bodies are phenomenologically indistinguishable.

Causal considerations, therefore, seem especially pertinent to the persistence conditions of material objects of any sort. Of course, the kinds of causal dependencies relating an object at earlier and later stages of its career will very likely differ according to the kind of object whose career we are tracing. Different kinds of persisting things will have different persistence conditions. What it is in virtue of which a human body persists is different from what it is in virtue of which a cupcake persists. But even so, causal considerations are relevant to the persistence of each.[11]

When it comes to the persistence of bodies, I suggest we think this way. Human bodies are like storms. A tornado, for example, picks up new stuff and throws off old stuff as it moves through space. Human bodies are like that. They are storms of atoms moving through space and time. They take on new stuff (through the digestion of food, for example) and throw off old stuff as they go. (I will leave it to your imagination to come up with the various ways bodies throw off old stuff.) A body persists in virtue of the fact that the atoms that are caught up in a life-preserving (causal) relation at one time pass on that life-preserving causal relation to successive swarms of atoms. My body has persisted into the present because the atoms that are caught up in the life of my body now have been bequeathed that life-preserving causal relation from the atoms that were caught up in its life a moment ago.[12]

We can name this condition on the persistence of human bodies the immanent causal condition, or ICC. In immanent causation, a state x of thing A brings about a consequent state y *in A itself*, whereas in cases of causation of the sort we normally think of, a thing A brings about state changes *in a numerically distinct thing*, B. For example, the state or event of a rock's hurtling through the air brings about state changes in the window it hits. ICC makes it a requirement on

---

11. See Chris Swoyer, "Causation and Identity," *Midwest Studies in Philosophy* 9 (1984): 593–622.

12. To put it a bit more technically: If an organism O that exists at t_2 is the same as an organism P that exists at t_1, and P *persisted* from t_1 to t_2, then the (set of) simples that compose P at t_1 must be causally related to the (set of) simples that compose O at t_2. Simples are whatever turn out to be the fundamental building blocks of physical objects.

the persistence of an organism that *immanent* causal relations hold among the different stages of an organism's career.[13]

So much for bodies. What of persons? What are their persistence conditions? I would argue that a *necessary* condition for the persistence of a person is that his or her constituting physical organism persists. If your body does not persist, then you do not persist. Not because you are your body, but because the existence of your body is necessary for your own persistence. What is both necessary and *sufficient* for personal survival is that *this* persisting physical organism preserve its capacity to subserve a range of intentional states, including a first-person perspective.

To this point, like nearly all accounts of the metaphysical nature of human persons in the analytic tradition of philosophy, even Christian accounts, mine has failed to mention a feature of personhood often emphasized in non-metaphysical accounts of human nature. The feature I have in mind is that of the essential *relationality* of persons. How does the feature of *persons-in-relation* fit with the Constitution View? I want to suggest that it fits quite well.

PERSONS-IN-RELATION

Metaphysical accounts of human nature are primarily interested in providing necessary and sufficient conditions for personhood. In other words, such accounts are almost exclusively interested in saying what it is in virtue of which some entity *is* a person. According to CV, something is a person if, and only if, it possesses a capacity for a first-person perspective. In order for something to be a *human* person, according to CV, it must have a body that it, and it alone, can refer to in a first-person way.

Christian tradition and Scripture itself, on the other hand, provide suggestive material for thinking that personhood and *relationality*

13. See Dean Zimmerman, "Immanent Causation," *Philosophical Perspectives* 11 (1997): 433–71; and also idem, "The Compatibility of Materialism and Survival," *Faith and Philosophy* 16 (1999): 194–212. Zimmerman offers the definition of "temporal-stage" for objects in general. I have taken the liberty of making relevant substitutions so that the definition applies to organisms in particular. Technically, we can put it this way: A human body B that exists at t_3 is the same as a human body A that exists at t_1, *in virtue of persisting from t_1 to t_3*, in the case that the temporal stages leading up to B at t_3 are immanent causally connected to the temporal stage of A at t_1.

are essentially linked. For example, the Christian tradition claims that God exists in *three* persons in intimate Trinitarian relation. And the account of the creation of human beings in Genesis 2 is equally suggestive. After many divine pronouncements of "it is good" following an act of divine creation, we read after the creation of the first human being, "it is *not* good. . . ." What is *not* good, of course, is that "man" should be *alone* on the earth. And so God creates an*other* human being for the first to stand in relation to. Even before the creation of another *human* being, the first human being appears in the Christian story already embedded in relationships of various sorts, relationship to God, to non-human animals, and to the rest of the biosphere. So according to the biblical narrative in Genesis, human beings make their first appearance already within the context of others. It is no exaggeration to say, therefore, that human persons are always—from the beginning of the Christian narrative to its very end—*persons-in-relation*. It is plausible to believe that this feature of the biblical narrative is eminently relevant to the issue of personhood.

Since CV makes no reference to relationality in its account of personhood, how is it that I can claim that CV fits the picture of *persons-in-relation* quite well? It is easier to see how this is so if we first distinguish the issue of *what* we are from the issue of *who* we are. With respect to what we are, it is plausible to believe that relationality is causally necessary for the emergence of a first-person perspective. In other words, it is plausible to believe that thinking of oneself as oneself without the need of a description or third-person pronoun (having a first-person perspective) requires a social and linguistic environment—it requires *others*. So, relationality is at minimum *causally* essential to the emergence of a first-person perspective.

However, when stating necessary and sufficient conditions for something's being a person (or an automobile or even an aardvark), it is common practice to leave out, or not to explicitly state, what plays an essential causal role in the coming to be of that thing. For example, among the necessary conditions for something's being a bicycle are the conditions that it have two wheels, be used for human transportation, and be propelled by human energy. Now, it is also true that there is a causal story involved in the coming to be of the wheels. Likely they were manufactured with the use of various tools and materials. Yet, what is causally required for the coming to be of the wheels does not show up in the list of conditions that are individually necessary and jointly sufficient for something's *being* a bicycle. That is because when we provide necessary and sufficient conditions we are usually providing *metaphysically* necessary and sufficient conditions and not *causally* necessary and sufficient conditions. So just because relationality does not show up in CV (an account of what is metaphysically necessary and sufficient for personhood) does not mean that it is not in some other important sense essential.

With respect to *who* we are, however, things are quite different. Here relations are front and center. A particular human person is *who* she is not just in virtue of having a first-person perspective or having a body that she, and she alone can refer to in a first person way. Rather there are many sorts of properties that make someone who she is. Some such properties are broadly *psychological*, like one's particular likes and dislikes, loves and hates, particular memories, particular hopes, etc. Other sorts of properties that make someone who she is are *dispositional*. For example, among the properties that made Mother Teresa of Calcutta who she was was her disposition to be compassionate, unselfish, and generous (i.e., her tendency to display those virtues in the relevant contexts). But not only was it the properties of compassion, unselfishness, and generosity but also the inimitable way Mother Teresa exercised those virtues that made Mother Teresa who she was.

My point here is to highlight the fact that many of the properties that make us who we are require a linguistic, social environment in order to be manifested and are relational in nature. They could not, in other words, have been exercised in introspective isolation nor could they have been exercised by a disembodied soul.

In short, not only the persons we become but also our very coming to be requires more than a biological organism with a network of neural circuitry of the requisite configurational complexity. It requires too a rich social environment. CV fits this picture of the ineluctably relational character of human personhood very well. It may not go as far as some would desire. For some may want to assert that relationality is not just *causally* necessary for *what* we are, and not just central to *who* we are, but some might wish to assert that relationality is in some deep sense *constitutive* of personhood. CV does not go that far, but it does take us quite a long way down the road of relationality and is, for that reason, preferable to other metaphysical views of personhood.

This concludes my positive account of the Constitution View of human persons. The Constitution View offers an account of human nature that makes good on the fundamental insight of dualism—we are *not* identical with human bodies. It also preserves a fundamental insight of animalism—we are *essentially* physical creatures that cannot possibly exist if our bodies don't exist. Moreover, as we have seen, it fits quite nicely with the claim that relationality is central to human personhood. What I want to do now is to consider some philosophical objections to CV. For much to my chagrin, CV has not taken the philosophical world by storm!

PHILOSOPHICAL OBJECTIONS TO THE CONSTITUTION VIEW

One objection to CV is based on a principle concerning part/whole relations. The claim is that there is a good argument for the view that if human persons are physical objects, then human persons must be identical with their bodies. The argument is based on what philosophers call mereological principles, where mereology is the study of part/whole relations. Let us say that x and y stand in the community of parts relation only if *every* material part of x is a material part of y and vice versa. Thus, it may seem that if x and y stand in the community of parts relation, then x = y. Am I identical with my body? The objection invites me simply to enumerate the material parts of me and the material parts of my body. If my body and I share all our material parts in common, we are identical. Since my body and I do in fact share all their material parts in common I *must be* identical with my body.

There are several problems with this argument. First, suppose we take a riding lawnmower and completely dismantle it, leaving before us a wide assortment of variously colored parts of all different shapes and sizes. Suppose we take those same parts, all of them, and after some bending and reconfiguring fashion out of them a go-kart. Surely the riding lawnmower is not identical with the go-kart, even though the two have all their material parts in common. Therefore, from the fact that x and y have all their material parts in common, it does not follow that x = y.

Suppose the objector says that his or her claim is that x = y only if x and y are composed of the same matter *at the same time* and not at different times. That will not do either. Anyone inclined to doubt that I am identical with my body is likely to doubt the condition. The reason is that the condition contradicts the plausible assumption that if x and y differ at *any* time, then x ≠ y.[14]

Another problem with this objection to CV is its use of the community of parts principle. The problem is twofold. First, as we have seen, it is plausible to believe that two things can share all their material parts in common without being identical, as was illustrated by our lawnmower example. Second, since a thing of one kind wholly constitutes a thing of a different kind only if every material part of the one is a material part of the other, constitution in fact *entails* sameness of material parts. It's not much of an objection to CV, in other words, to point out what defenders of the view tout as an *entailment* of the view. One may want to raise a question concerning the counting of parts based on what I have just said. For example, if my body and I share all our parts, then just how many heads are there where my head is located? I have a head, and my body has a head. Doesn't 1 + 1 = 2? Yet there is only one head where CV would lead us to believe there are two. I'll deal with such objections shortly. All I want to do here is to claim that if x and y stand in the community of parts relation, this by itself does not entail that x = y.

Even so, we must admit that this central entailment of constitution, (that numerically distinct physical objects can wholly fill the same spatial boundaries) is counterintuitive. Still, I think the arguments for the nonidentity of constituting and constituted thing are sufficiently compelling to warrant accepting them. Moreover, it is worth pointing out that constitution seems only to force this *one* counterintuitive consequence, whereas other materialist views seem to proliferate counterintuitive consequences.[15] Of course, some philosophers have objected that, on the contrary, scores of counterintuitive puzzles are entailed by constitution. To rebut this sort of response, I want to consider three puzzles that a constitution account of persons allegedly engenders and raise one theological objection concerning the *imago Dei*.

14. The assumption is plausible given that identity is a relation that each thing *necessarily* stands in to itself. If x = y, then it is necessary that x = y. And if x = y is necessary, then it is not possible that x and y differ. If x = y, then x = y at any and all times.

15. See my "Persons, Bodies, and the Constitution Relation," *Southern Journal of Philosophy* 37 (1999): 1–20.

Multiplying Parts, Vanishing Weight, Multiplying Objects, and the Incarnation

The Puzzle of Multiplying Parts

In response to the part/whole objection, I claimed that if x constitutes y, then x and y have all their parts in common. But I also claim that I am constituted by my body. My body has a left index finger as a part. By the principle entailed by constitution, it would seem that I too have a left index finger. But if I am not identical with my body, then it follows that there are two left index fingers where my left index finger is. But that is absurd.

I respond this way. The relationship that I claim holds between me and my body is constitution. The relationship that holds between my left index finger and my body's left index finger is identity. Constitution does not entail that two physical things *of the same kind* can simultaneously spatially coincide. In fact, it denies it. Since my left index finger and my body's left index finger are of the same kind (they are both fingers) and occupy precisely the same place at the same time, they are not related by constitution but by identity.

The Puzzle of Vanishing Weight

Here is a similar complaint. It seems that both my body and I weigh the same. But if my body weighs 130 pounds and I do too, then why doesn't the scale register 260 pounds when I stand on it? One philosopher refers to this puzzle as the problem of vanishing weight and believes that the problem is a devastating one for defenders of constitution. I disagree.

If I weigh 130 pounds, then so does my constituting body, *and so does the sum*, me + my body. The sum me + my body, has a weight of only 130 pounds, since every complete decomposition of me + my body is 130 pounds. In other words, my body can be decomposed in terms of cells, molecules, or even atoms. But I do not discover the mass of my body by first discovering the weight of cells and adding that to the weight of atoms. Rather, the mass of my body is gotten by taking the mass of just one complete decomposition of it.

Let me put it another way. Parthood is transitive (i.e., if cells are parts of my leg and my leg is a part of my body, then cells are parts of my body). Suppose that among my leg's parts are a bunch of cells, and suppose that among the parts of the cells are a bunch of atoms.

If parthood is transitive, then the atoms are parts of my leg. Suppose now that both bunches are complete decompositions of my leg. Then the weight of the cells is *identical with* the weight of the atoms. Therefore, the mass of whatever fills a particular spatial region is not determined by adding together the masses of *all* of the objects that fill that region. Rather, the mass of an object is determined by adding together the masses of one complete decomposition of that object. Therefore, there is no mystery involving vanishing weight, since no weight somehow mysteriously vanishes. Once it is realized that my body and I share the same matter, the puzzle dissolves.

The Puzzle of Multiplying Objects

One may still insist that the constitution theorist has counting problems. For example, take the thought I have that winters in Grand Rapids are agonizingly long and unpleasant. How many thinkers are having just that thought in the nearest vicinity of my physical organism? Mustn't the constitution theorist say that there are at least two: me and the physical organism that constitutes me? Since my act of thinking the thoughts I do seems crucially to involve my brain, so the objection goes, it would seem that my physical organism is a good candidate for thinking thoughts. But isn't it odd that there should be two thinkers thinking all of the thoughts I have ever thought or will ever think?[16]

That would indeed be odd. Thankfully, a Constitution View of persons does not commit me to it. As I said earlier, *persons* think thoughts, presumably in virtue of having brains of certain sorts, just as human agents perform certain actions, presumably in virtue of having limbs of certain sorts. Just as brains are not the thinkers of thoughts but people are, it is likewise true that physical organisms are not the thinkers of thoughts. Human persons think thoughts in virtue of being constituted by physical organisms of a certain physical complexity. It is wrong to suggest that one's physical organism is a good candidate for thinking thoughts just as it is wrong to suggest that my body is a good candidate for the blameworthiness of some action. The relevant objects in the case of moral evaluations are

16. This problem is raised by Michael Burke, "Preserving the Principle of One Object to a Place," *Philosophy and Phenomenological Research* 3 (1994): 621. See also van Inwagen, *Material Beings*, 126–27; and Dean Zimmerman, "Theories of Masses and Problems of Constitution," *The Philosophical Review* 104 (1995): 88.

agents; the relevant objects in the case of thinkers are people, not the physical organisms that constitute them.[17]

The Puzzle of the Incarnation

One may ask how a Christian materialist can possibly explain the incarnation. The putative problem is this. If God (or the Second Person of the Trinity) is *essentially* an immaterial being, then how could such a being become *purely* material without losing an essential property? If the Second Person of the Trinity loses an *essential* property, then wouldn't he cease to be fully God?

I believe CV actually offers a way of understanding the dual natures of Christ that is somewhat more plausible than that offered by Substance Dualism. According to the Chalcedonian formulation, the incarnate Christ is one person with two natures, a fully divine nature (that of the Second Person of the Trinity) and a fully human nature (that of Jesus of Nazareth). CV divides things where one would expect—between the human nature and the divine nature of the single person. Keep in mind that the *person* of Christ is *not* human; he is divine, being the Second Person of the Trinity. But this one person, in the incarnation, had two natures—human and divine. According to this understanding of the dual natures, Christ is *wholly* immaterial in his divine nature and *wholly* material in his human nature. Consider the less than elegant cleavage Substance Dualists must offer. According to Substance Dualism, Christ is wholly immaterial in his divine nature and partly material and partly immaterial in his human nature. Therefore, in my mind, CV, far from being unable to accommodate the doctrine of the incarnation, is actually better able to explain the doctrine than is dualism.

Before moving on, notice two things. First, it is a veritable mystery how a single entity can be both fully divine and fully human. It is no less a mystery for dualism than for materialism. Second, notice the mistake that was made in framing the original objection to CV. The objection was that CV requires that the Second Person of the Trinity, an *essentially* immaterial person, became *purely* material in the incarnation. But if that is so, then the Second Person of the Trinity ceases to be God. If what I said above is true, however, the Second

---

17. The objection could be pressed further in terms of the doctrine known as microphysical supervenience. I addressed this line of objection in "Persons, Bodies, and the Constitution Relation," 14–17.

Person of the Trinity did not become *purely* material (or even *partly* material). The Second *Person* of the Trinity did not give up immateriality in the incarnation. Remember: he was one person (divine and immaterial) with not one but, in the incarnation, *two* natures—one immaterial, the other material. How can that be? I do not know, but the mystery of the incarnation is not explained away by any account, be it dualist or materialist.

What about the Imago Dei?

If it is true that we human persons are wholly material beings, as CV claims, then what does it mean to say we are created in God's image? Doesn't being created in the image of God just mean having an immaterial soul and the features of intellect, will, and emotion that characterize soul? As mentioned in chapter 2, I do not believe that our being created in the image of God means that we are immaterial as God is immaterial. What then *does* it mean?

There are many ways we human beings image God. Among them are the following. First, we image God when we care for creation and contribute to the terrestrial flourishing of the created order. This is what the Bible means when it speaks of our having been given dominion. We are God's vice-regents, as it were. To have dominion is to care for others, including nonhuman others such as oceans and streams, octopuses and salamanders. In other words, to have dominion is to tend to the well-being of all the earth. Second, we image God when we live in loving relation to other human beings and invest ourselves in their flourishing and well-being. This ties back, of course, to the previous discussion of the theological insight that we are essentially persons-in-relation. Since God is a Trinity, it is not surprising that we should image God in social and not just individual ways. The tenor of the relationship between the three persons of the Trinity is one of a harmonious and free exchange of love and joy. Therefore, engaging in acts of mercy, hospitality, love, kindness, and so on is to act like God. In fact, we image God when we image Jesus, who welcomed the outcast, fed the hungry, clothed the naked, hated evil, and delighted in doing the work of the Father. Finally, we also image God in our suffering. God is love. To love is to open ourselves up to suffering. When we lay down our lives for our friends, and yes, our enemies too, we image God, who laid down his life for us in Jesus.

None of these ways that we image God rules out the fact that we are wholly material beings. None implies it either. But the fact that we are created in the image of God is perfectly compatible with the claim that we are material beings. Indeed, nothing in the doctrine of the *imago Dei*, rightly understood, entails a dualist view of human nature.

CONCLUSION

The constitution account of human nature provides an alternative to animalism, on the one hand, and dualism, on the other. This chapter tried to answer some typical philosophical objections (and one kind of theological objection) to this view of human persons. It did not, I admit, answer all types of objections. In particular, this chapter did not address certain theological and moral objections to the view. For example, according to CV, human bodies come into existence before human persons do and can even outlive the persons they constitute. What kind of moral consequences does such a view have for beginning of life ethical questions? Moreover, according to CV, human persons are essentially constituted by the bodies that constitute them. But bodies apparently give out, die, and cease to exist. What consequences does such a view have for the Christian hope of postmortem existence? In the next two chapters I address these questions.

4

The Stem Cell Challenge

THIS CHAPTER IS DIVIDED INTO three sections. In the first section I defend the Constitution View of persons against charges that it has horrendous moral implications. I show that neither Metaphysical Materialism nor Metaphysical Dualism all by itself either entails or precludes an ethic of life. Thus, in the second section I supplement the Constitution View of persons with a theology of embodiment. I show how the doctrines of creation, incarnation, and resurrection all point to the value of materiality and embodiment. Then, in the third section I tease out some implications of these doctrines for the ethical issues of stem cell research, human cloning, and other reproductive technologies after first exploring the early stages of embryonic development and some details of human embryonic stem cell extraction.

METAPHYSICS AND MORALITY

The Putative Problem Stated

According to the Constitution View presented in the last chapter, human persons are essentially physical *and* essentially psychological. One implication of this view is that no early term fetus constitutes a person. Another implication is that any entity once possessing but having lost *all* capacity for the relevant kinds of psychological states also fails to constitute a person. Therefore, human organisms in irreversible and persistent vegetative states (PVS) no longer constitute persons. According to animalism, on the other hand, human persons are essentially *animals* and only contingently *persons*. In fact, according to animalists, you and I were once human *nonpersons* as fetuses, and, if things should go badly for us, we may one day be human nonpersons again (e.g., if we should ever be PVS patients with completely destroyed cerebra).[1]

Among the objections to *materialist* views[2] of human persons, like animalism and the Constitution View, are two that concern alleged ethical implications. These two objections, however, are rarely distinguished. So let me distinguish them. One objection is that materialist views are defective because they lack the metaphysical resources to generate moral obligations or moral expectations to protect life in either its early or late stages. In other words, we want a metaphysical view of persons to have this positive moral implication, and materialist views like CV lack it. Another objection relies on the claim that our metaphysical view of human persons is decisive for "virtually every debated issue in biomedical ethics today"[3] and that any view according to which some human organisms lack the property of personhood has horrendous moral implications. Put another way, the positive moral implications CV *does have* are horrible.

I acknowledge that materialist views of human persons like CV do fail to provide *metaphysical* resources necessary or sufficient for generating moral obligations or moral expectations to protect and care for the life of a human fetus or a PVS patient. However, *any* metaphysical view of persons, be that metaphysic dualist or materialist in nature, is impotent to provide such resources. Other resources, metaphysically

1. See Eric Olson, *The Human Animal* (Ithaca: Cornell University Press, 1999); and idem, "Was I Ever a Fetus?" *Philosophy and Phenomenological Research* 57 (1997): 95–110.

2. Remember that I am using the term *materialist* in such a way that it is not incompatible with Christian theism. That is, I mean to limit materialism in this discussion to metaphysical views of *human* persons. According to such views, therefore, human persons are *wholly* physical objects. This claim is perfectly compatible, of course, with the claim that there are nonhuman persons (e.g., God and the angels) that are immaterial.

3. J. P. Moreland and Scott Rae, *Body and Soul: Human Nature and the Crisis in Ethics* (Downers Grove, IL: InterVarsity, 2000), 236.

neutral with respect to dualism and materialism, must be added to such views to generate moral obligations or moral expectations to care for and protect human life. Indeed, accounts of human persons entailing that some human organisms are not also persons do not have the horrible ethical implications they are alleged to have. In fact, and most surprising, dualism itself is compatible with, and in some cases even entails, the claim that abortion does not end the existence of a human person, and therefore any prohibition against abortion cannot be based on the belief that an abortion destroys a person.

The Problem Explained

The most recent and explicit statement that one's metaphysics of persons is decisive for the ethical issues of abortion and euthanasia appears in J. P. Moreland and Scott Rae's *Body and Soul*. Moreland and Rae argue for "the relevance of our philosophical reflections on human personhood to many of the most intensely debated moral issues of the day,"[4] and they also "point out the ethical implications of our philosophical view of a human person."[5] They argue that the philosophical materialist account of persons, and what they call the Christian complementarian account of persons, have "serious, troublesome implications for the ethical issues [of abortion, fetal research, cloning, and physician-assisted suicide]."[6] They seem to believe that only a Substance Dualist view of human persons can deliver the needed resources for a viable ethic of life. Any view of human persons according to which some human organisms are not also persons "opens the door" to the mistreatment of those at the edges of life, both fetuses and patients in persistent vegetative states.[7]

The argument appears to be as follows:

1. According to materialist conceptions of persons, human personhood is grounded in the possession of certain kinds of psychological properties or the capacity for them.
2. If human personhood is grounded in the possession of psychological properties or the capacity for them, then some human organisms fail to instantiate the property of being a person.

4. Ibid., 231.
5. Ibid.
6. Ibid., 87–88.
7. Ibid., 255.

3. If a human organism fails to instantiate the property of being a person, then that organism lacks a moral status sufficient for generating moral obligations or moral expectations to care for and protect its life.
4. Therefore, according to materialist conceptions of persons, some human organisms (e.g., early term human fetuses) fail to instantiate the property of being a person.
5. Therefore, according to materialist conceptions of persons, some human organisms lack a moral status sufficient for generating moral obligations or moral expectations to protect their lives.

It is, I believe, on the basis of such a conclusion as 5 that some are erroneously led to conclude that materialist conceptions of persons have the following troublesome implication, namely, that we have *no* moral obligations or responsibilities with respect to nonperson-constituting human organisms.

The argument to premise 5 is logically valid. Although questions can be raised about other premises, I want to focus here on the third premise. Those in the Moreland and Rae camp must give good reasons for accepting premise 3. Moreland and Rae themselves do not. They fail to establish a connection between a so-called materialist conception of persons and the morality of abortion, some varieties of euthanasia, fetal research, and human cloning. In chapter 3 of *Body and Soul*, they assert that such a connection exists, describe the metaphysics of materialism as it relates to persons, and then reassert the connection at the end of the chapter. But nowhere in the chapter or elsewhere in the book is the alleged connection established.

The intuition that I suspect may be motivating Moreland and Rae is one that I believe is fairly widespread. It can be expressed as a necessary condition for grounding our obligations to the unborn and other vulnerable human lives. Call it INTUITION.

INTUITION: A necessary condition for grounding our obligations to the unborn and other vulnerable human lives is a commitment to the belief that human persons have immaterial souls.

Supplementing INTUITION with another claim we'll call SOUL

SOUL: The CV of personhood denies that human persons have immaterial souls.

delivers what admittedly would be, if true, a defect in CV. For what it delivers is a claim we'll call OBLIGATION.

OBLIGATION: A CV of personhood lacks the requisite resources for grounding our obligations to the unborn and other vulnerable human lives.

The idea that INTUITION attempts to capture is that there is a very tight connection between personhood and moral status such that anything lacking personhood lacks a moral status sufficient to guarantee a prohibition against its killing. Given INTUITION, and accepting SOUL, seems to commit the defender of CV to the claim that we have no moral obligations or responsibilities with respect to protecting the life of nonperson-constituting human organisms.

The problem, however, is that although the move to OBLIGATION from INTUITION and SOUL is valid, INTUITION is neither intuitively known nor self-evidently true. I believe it is not only not obviously true but also demonstrably false. Indeed, I want to show that dualism is not only not necessary for generating obligations and responsibilities to fetuses and PVS patients but also compatible with the belief that no abortion ends the existence of a human person.

Why Metaphysics Is Not Enough

If I am correct, then at the root of Moreland and Rae's argument is the intuition that a necessary condition for grounding our obligations to the unborn and other vulnerable human lives is the fact that persons are or have immaterial, substantial souls. If that intuition is true, then the following two claims cannot both be true:

1. Human persons are necessarily, wholly material things.
2. Abortion is morally wrong.

It seems obvious, however, that materialists can be committed to the moral *impermissibility* of abortion. This "seeming" does not itself establish the compatibility of the couplet of claims above, but I think it does suggest that Metaphysical Dualism about persons is not essential or necessary for generating a moral obligation or moral expectation to protect human life. For ease of discussion, I will refer to the moral obligation or moral expectation to protect human life as constituting an ethic of life. To see how a metaphysics of materialism about persons is compatible with an ethic of life, consider the following.

Suppose human persons are human organisms with developed capacities for the rich sort of psychological life normally associated with adult human beings (i.e., suppose human persons are *necessarily* psychological beings). If so, then no early term human fetus is a person. Surely, however, one with such a view of human persons could coherently protest the abortion of an early term fetus on the grounds that (1) it is *prima facie* morally wrong to destroy a person *in potentia*, and a normal human fetus is just such a being, or (2) even if the fetus is defective and does not qualify as a potential person, it is still a member of the *human* community, and to terminate the existence of a member of the community would diminish the kind of bond essential to the preservation and health of the community.[8]

Notice that in each of the reasons just offered for prohibiting the abortion of an early term fetus the metaphysics of persons was supplemented with *moral principles* to yield the moral conclusion. I suggest that this is not just a fact about metaphysical materialism about persons or the particular reasons chosen but a fact about the insufficiency of any metaphysical view of personhood all by itself to ground an ethic of life. I should also hasten to point out that each of the reasons offered is eminently plausible as a *prima facie* justification for prohibiting the destruction of a human nonperson.

Consider now the claim that human persons are at least partially composed of immaterial souls, which are connected as intimately as you like to human organisms. According to all such dualist views currently offered by Christian philosophers, be it the Substance Dualism of Descartes examined in chapter 1 or the Compound Dualism advocated by Moreland and Rae, be it Emergent Dualism or Creationist Dualism, it is metaphysically possible for the soul both (1) to continue in existence after the demise of the organism it animates and (2) to carry with it the identity of the person. According to such views, therefore, abortion ends the life of an object that is such that if it ceases to exist no person will cease to exist as

---

8. Even if we distinguish between the *biologically human* community and the *morally human* community, such that strictly speaking human fetuses are members of the former but not members of the latter, it is still plausible to believe that to terminate the existence of a member of the former is to diminish the kind of bond essential to the preservation and health of the latter.

a result. For this reason, it is not only plausible to think that abortion never ends the existence of a person, it is in fact an entailment of Moreland and Rae's own brand of dualism. And if an abortion never ends the existence of a person, then, for dualists, any prohibition against abortion cannot be based on the fact that abortion destroys a person.[9] According to such a view as Moreland and Rae's, one can still oppose abortion, of course. One may, for example, offer the following as support for a prohibition against abortion:

> God intends every human person to be a soul-body composite, and abortion is the wrenching apart of what God intends to be joined.

Notice, however, that the metaphysics of dualism *alone* does not support the moral conclusion that the life of a human fetus ought to be protected. Instead, it is an appeal to God's intentions that, coupled with the metaphysics, supports the prohibition. But such a consideration is no less congenial to materialist views of persons, as I will soon suggest. I believe that our discussion so far is sufficient to demonstrate that neither a metaphysics of dualism nor a metaphysics of naturalism *alone* settles the moral issues at stake by either entailing or precluding an ethic of life. I conclude, therefore, that although it is true that materialist views of persons lack the metaphysical resources either necessary or sufficient to generate moral obligations or moral expectations to prohibit the taking of human life, this is also true of dualist views of persons.

Some Objections and Replies

Objection: Some may object that materialist views of persons are not all on a par and that even if *some* versions of materialism do not have horrendous moral implications, it is not the case that *all* do not. For example, consider animalism. According to animalists, although every human person was once an early term human fetus, no early term human fetus is a human *person*. Therefore, every human person once was, and may be again, a human *nonperson*. Yet granting the moral principle that "a killing is the loss to the victim of the value of

9. If a dualist objects that a living human fetus *is* a person in virtue of being ensouled, then I don't understand how a thing (a person) can become identical with a part of itself (i.e., a soul).

its future,"[10] it follows that aborting human but nonpersonal fetuses would be *prima facie* seriously morally wrong. It would be wrong because to abort them would be to deprive them of valuable futures, namely, futures just like ours.[11]

But now consider CV, articulated in the last chapter. It seems to be handicapped in ways animalism is not. For, according to CV, human persons are not identical with human animals. Therefore, it appears as though defenders of CV cannot avail themselves of a moral principle like "a wrong making feature of a killing is the loss to the victim of the value of its future." They cannot avail themselves of a principle like this, it may be argued, since, according to CV, none of us human persons is, was, or ever will be numerically identical with a human animal, including human fetuses. Since no human fetus is, was, or ever will be identical with a human person, killing a human fetus will not deprive the fetus of a personal future. So it might be objected that CV in particular is without the resources to ground a plausible ethic of life.[12]

Reply: Defenders of CV possess the resources needed to ground a plausible ethic of life. First, as I've pointed out, we are not, in the ordinary business of life, given to distinguishing the "is" of identity from the "is" of constitution. Am I a human animal? Was I ever a

10. Don Marquis "Why Abortion Is Immoral," *Journal of Philosophy* 86 (1989): 192.

11. See Peter van Inwagen, *Material Beings* (Ithaca: Cornell University Press, 1990); and Olsen, *Human Animal*, for animalist views of human persons.

12. It is worth pointing out that according to some readings of Aquinas human ensoulment does not occur until around the third month of gestation. Therefore, prior to the third month there is no human being in the womb, since where there is no *human soul*, there is no human being. Thus, the nonhuman "transitional beings" that exist in the womb prior to human ensoulment also will not become human beings. Rather, they will be replaced by human beings and will have been composed of the very same stuff that composes the human beings that eventually take their place. So a similar objection applies even to certain interpretations of Compound Dualism. Of course, this is not an insurmountable problem if the basic thesis of this chapter is correct. For discussions of Thomist embryology, see Brian Leftow, "Souls Dipped in Dust," in *Soul, Body, and Survival: Essays on the Metaphysics of Human Persons*, ed. Kevin Corcoran (Ithaca: Cornell University Press, 2001), 120–38. Christina van Dyke addresses the issue of Aquinas's embryology in "Aquinas on Human Bodies, Persons, and the End of Life" (under review). See also William Wallace, "Aquinas's Legacy on Individuation, Cogitation, and Homonization," in *Thomas Aquinas and His Legacy*, ed. David Gallagher (Washington, DC: Catholic University of America Press, 1994), 173–93.

human fetus? Defenders of CV say yes to both. I am a human animal in the sense that I am now *constituted by* a human animal that once was a fetus. As a defender of CV, therefore, I could employ some of the same kinds of moral principles animalists use to generate prohibitions against abortion. For example, because a normal human fetus is a person *in potentia*, in the sense that it will come to constitute a person if left to develop in the ordinary way, the life of a human fetus ought to be protected. In the same way, even if the fetus is defective and does not qualify as a potential person, in the sense that there is no likelihood that it will come to constitute a person, it is still a member of the biologically human community, and to terminate the existence of a member of that community would diminish the kind of bond essential to the preservation and health of the *morally* human community.

Moreover, I have argued that *every* human fetus is created by God with the ultimate intention of coming to constitute a person, and on the basis of God's ultimately good intentions for it, there is a *prima facie* obligation to care for the life of the fetus.[13] The same holds for human organisms in persistent vegetative states. Indeed, it is plausible to believe that God intends for every human animal to constitute a person, and in view of this, there is a *prima facie* obligation not to kill a PVS patient. Therefore, even advocates of CV are not without the moral and theological resources to argue for the moral wrongness of aborting human fetuses. Although I believe such a move is sufficient to ward off charges against CV, I present in the next section a more fully developed theological vision available to the constitutionalist that makes the protection and preservation of human life morally required of us.

Objection: On the face of it, it looks as though a prohibition against killing a human fetus would be based on the fact that doing so would prevent it from coming to constitute a person or, in the case of human animals in persistent vegetative states, coming *again* to constitute a person, thus preempting God's intentions for the human animal.[14] However, based on a plausible principle of persistence for human bodies that I will present in the next chapter, it turns out that it is *possible* for human bodies to persist through death and also possible for their bodies to be resurrected some time after death. But if God

13. See my "Persons and Bodies," *Faith and Philosophy* 15 (1998): 324–40.
14. This objection was raised by William Hasker in correspondence.

sees to it that fetal bodies and the bodies of PVS patients do not go out of existence but persist through their deaths, or go out of existence only temporarily (only to be resurrected by God at some time in the future), the prohibition against killing cannot owe to preempting God's intentions. For if what I will argue in chapter 5 is correct, those intentions will be fulfilled, if not before death then after.

Reply: Whether God intervenes to resurrect our bodies or to see them remain intact through death, it does not follow that either of these gracious acts in any way diminishes our obligation not to kill. First, consider an analogy for resurrection. It would be wrong for my son to attempt to destroy the table I made even though, let us suppose, it is true that I could and would restore the table. It would be wrong for my son to take actions purposefully intended to destroy the table because, aside from a flagrant act of disrespect, it would, if successful, temporarily thwart the aims and intentions I had as its creator. It would cause the table to cease to exist, if not forever then at least for a time. So too with acts of killing human animals. Although God can and will raise human bodies from the dead, killing them would be at cross purposes with God's aims.

Consider now the case of intermediate survival. If our bodies can survive death, it is still plausible to believe that we have an obligation not to undertake actions that, save for the gracious intervention of God, would kill a human animal, since our undertaking such actions would be at cross purposes with God's intentions for natural, biological human life (i.e., they would, save for the gracious intervention of God, destroy what is necessary for human personhood, the end for which God creates human, biological life). So even if one is a materialist who believes as I do that though we die yet shall we live, either in virtue of being resurrected or persisting through death, there are still plausible reasons for the existence of a *prima facie* obligation not to kill.

Objection: Greg Ganssle has suggested that I imply that Moreland and Rae think moral obligations are all or nothing affairs. If a position does not protect the fetus to the same degree that it protects a fully functioning normal adult, then it offers *no protection at all*. Ganssle does not believe Moreland and Rae hold this view. According to Ganssle,

> The question of what constitutes adequate protection is one that gets its bite from moral dilemmas. It is relatively easy to have an ethic that

protects a fetus or a dog or a city park. The difficult questions come
in when *prima facie* obligations come into conflict with other *prima
facie* obligations. Do we keep the park or build adequate housing for
the inhabitants of the city? Ethical dilemmas involve the tug of competing claims. Which of the claimants deserves greater consideration
and protection?[15]

Therefore, as Ganssle sees it, the important question is not whether
we have obligations to human fetuses and adult human beings but, assuming we do, to which do we have greater obligation? Here is where
our metaphysics of persons makes a difference, thinks Ganssle.

Reply: It seems to me that Moreland and Rae say nothing in their
book that would lead one to believe that they hold the more nuanced
view that Ganssle believes they do. In the next section, however, I consider a thesis to which they may be committed that raises the very issues
Ganssle has his eye on. As I make clear in the section, I agree that what
counts as a person or a nonperson makes a difference in how we settle
moral issues. My argument to this point has been to establish the more
modest thesis that neither a metaphysics of dualism nor a metaphysics
of materialism all by itself either entails or precludes an ethic of life.

On the Word Person

One final issue remains to be discussed in this part of the chapter. I have been using the term *person* in the sense of an individual
with a capacity for certain kinds of psychological states. There are,
however, different senses of the term *person*. Suppose that instead of
using the term in my sense we use the term in the moral sense of an
entity deserving protection under an ethic of life (an entity possessing
inherent value). If we embrace a thesis like the following

MORAL BEINGS: Only human persons are moral beings (entities deserving
protection in virtue of possessing inherent value).

it may be thought that, while we have obligations toward nonpersons,
our obligations toward moral persons differ in important respects
from our obligations toward nonpersons. For example, obligations
toward moral persons are correlated with moral rights, and in virtue

15. See his "Metaphysics, Ethics, and Personhood: A Reply to Kevin Corcoran,"
Faith and Philosophy 22 (July 2005): 373.

of this, we may think our obligations toward persons are weightier than those toward nonpersons. If Moreland and Rae are committed to something like MORAL BEINGS, then they are right to think that views like animalism and CV, which deny personhood to early term human fetuses, cannot generate moral obligations that carry anything near the same weight as those generated by views that do count human fetuses as persons. Therefore, when moral obligations to human fetuses conflict with moral obligations to persons, obligations to persons trump those to human fetuses.

There are several ways to respond to this. First, I believe a virtue of grounding value in something like God's ultimately good intentions for creation is that one need tell only one story that obligates us to protect the life of created, living things, whereas a view like Moreland and Rae's must tell two stories: one of them yielding obligations to persons and another yielding obligations to nonpersons. Second, a single story grounding value in theistic intentions is compatible with different degrees of moral weightiness. Obligations to moral persons do seem weightier than obligations to nonpersons based on God's intentions for each kind. But it is plausible to believe that obligations to human nonpersons are, for the same reason, weightier than obligations to nonhuman nonpersons. For example, because God intends every human animal to constitute a human person, and human persons have a privileged role in God's economy, an obligation to human fetuses is weightier than an obligation to nonhuman entities, so much so as to prohibit the killing of human fetuses. For this reason, it follows that obligations to the mother (herself a person) of an early term human fetus are weightier than our obligations to the fetus. And I should hasten to point out here that even if human fetuses are counted as persons, as they are in the dualist view of Moreland and Rae, the moral dilemma is no easier to resolve. I believe, therefore, that materialist views of human persons like animalism and CV can grant MORAL BEINGS without any dire ethical consequences.

Summary

I have been arguing against the claim that a metaphysics of persons alone is decisive for an ethic of life. Neither a metaphysics of dualism nor a metaphysics of materialism alone either entails or precludes an ethic of life. I have also argued that views according to which some human organisms are not also persons are compatible with the belief that it is morally *impermissible* to kill human nonpersons. Where it may appear that a particular metaphysics of persons alone entails a particular moral conclusion (be that conclusion for or against life), it is instead other claims supplemental to it and conjoined with it that lead to the conclusion.

I believe that I have successfully shown that a robust ethic of life is congenial to materialist views of human persons. I have not settled, nor have I attempted to settle, *specific* moral dilemmas involving what to do when obligations to human fetuses conflict with our obligations to their mothers. That is a project better left to others more qualified than I. Even if I have been successful in showing that a robust ethic of life is congenial to materialist views of human persons, I have not yet presented what I think is the most important and persuasive case for an ethic of life. The next part of this chapter does just that.

CREATION, INCARNATION, AND RESURRECTION

In the introduction to this book I called attention to the fact that the church has historically and resolutely taken a stand against the antimaterialism of Marcion and his followers. Marcion's antimaterialism led him to reject the doctrine of the incarnation of God in Christ.[16] The church, in contrast to Marcion, is committed to three interrelated doctrines, a recovery of which holds tremendous promise in helping us think through beginning of life ethical issues such as embryonic stem cell research. The doctrines I have in mind are those of creation, incarnation, and resurrection. It is in the context of these doctrines that I wish to articulate a robust ethic of life. The purpose of this section is not to argue against dualism. Rather, the purpose is to provide a theological framework for considering ethical questions related to personhood.

Creation

We begin with the doctrine of creation. In the beginning, Scripture tells us, God created (Gen. 1). Although creation is not exhausted

---

16. I do not mean to imply here that Cartesian Dualists, Compound Dualists, Emergent Dualists, and constitution theorists are at odds with respect to embracing the doctrines of creation, incarnation, and resurrection. I do mean that Marcionism, a dualism that entails the devaluation of the material, is at odds with those relevant doctrines.

by the material creation (angels are created beings after all), it is the material world whose creation is chronicled in the opening pages of Genesis. And the story of creation is not merely a story of divine production or origination. It is a story of divine *delight*, delight in the material world brought into being by the Word. For upon creation, it is as though God steps back to survey his work and, over and over again, pronounces his blessing upon the fruit of his labor. The creational refrain, "It is good!" echoes throughout the pages of Genesis and beyond. So, the doctrine of creation includes the *goodness* of creation (Gen. 1:31), the initial divine affirmation of materiality and embodiment (John 1:10).

There is more, of course, to the doctrine of creation than creation's goodness and God's delight. In Old Testament terms, everything is created by the God who called Israel into covenantal relationship and to whom Israel relates as God's chosen. God the Creator is not only sovereign and powerful but also reliable and trustworthy. Says one commentator, for Israel, "creation is the fundamental ground for a reflected dependence, trust, thankfulness, and obedience to God" (Pss. 103:22; 119:73; Isa. 17:2; 22:11; 40:26–31).[17] In other words, built into the doctrine of creation are the notions of *gift, creaturely dependence,* and *vocation.* The creation, including human beings, is a product of love, of divine giving. As creation, all that exists depends on God for its continued existence. Creation is not *self*-existent; it has its source of being in the God on whom it depends. The *vocation* of God's human creatures consists in their call to acknowledge their dependence on God, the good Creator, and to respond in gratitude, trust, and obedience.

It is tempting to think that the fall of human beings, and the twisting, distorting, and obscuring of creation that resulted, erased the goodness and divine affirmation of materiality and embodiment. But this is not so. Recall the words of Paul in Romans:

> For the creation waits with eager longing for the revealing of the children of God; for the creation was subjected to futility, not of its own will but by the will of the one who subjected it, in hope, that the creation itself will be set free from its bondage to decay and will obtain the freedom of the glory of the children of God. We know that the whole creation has been groaning in labor pains until now; and

17. Luc Richard, OMI, "Christology and Creation," *Word and Spirit* 5 (1983): 31.

not only the creation, but we ourselves, who have the first fruits of
the Spirit, groan inwardly while we wait for adoption, the redemption
of our bodies.

8:19–23

In other words, in keeping with Israel's trust in the faithfulness of God
the Creator, the New Testament writers remained confident in God's
covenantal love and care for the material or embodied world God had
brought into being. God did not abandon it on account of sin. No!
God so loves and cares for the world formed by his hands that he has
enacted a drama of rescue, a drama of truly cosmic scope; it is a drama
that has at its core *materiality* and *embodiment*. As one author puts it,
"From the virgin's womb to Joseph's tomb the saving story is a human
biography with a body."[18]

Incarnation and Resurrection

The incarnation, the taking on of flesh by the Second Person of
the Trinity, signals God's *re*-affirmation of embodiment and creation.
The doctrines of creation and incarnation are intimately connected.
Jesus of Nazareth is identified with the Creator of the world insofar
as he is understood in New Testament terms as the divine Word
(John 1:1–5) through whose power and rule the world was created.
He is the beginning of creation (Col. 1:15) and, at the same time, the
rightful heir to creation insofar as all things were created through him
and for him. And let us not forget that the incarnation of the Second
Person of the Trinity, his taking on of flesh, was neither momentary
nor provisional. God's persistent "yes" to embodiment reverberates
into eternity in the resurrection, exaltation, and glorification of the
embodied Christ. In the next chapter I take up the possibility of resurrection given a materialist metaphysics of persons. Here I just want
to emphasize the importance of the doctrine in terms of embodiment.
The humanity of Christ, his embodied nature, is not shed in the new
Jerusalem. It is taken up, exalted, and glorified.

This brings us to yet another element of the creation-incarnation-
resurrection motif that is relevant to beginning of life ethical issues.
The perspective of the New Testament is that Jesus, the second Adam,

---

18. Todd Murken, "The Exalted Humanity of the Ascended Christ: Food for the
World," *Currents in Theology and Mission* 21 (1994): 274–83, especially 281.

is the *destiny* of creation and the human race in particular. It is he, the second Adam, who restores creation and recaptures the *imago Dei* in which the first Adam had been created. In his resurrection and glorification, humanity realizes its nature, the end for which it was created.

In a free and loving act, God created us for free and loving relationship with himself as Creator. In Jesus of Nazareth, the second Adam, creation finally succeeded in its call to free, loving, and trusting relationship with God. This is important. Jesus Christ, the very incarnation of the Second Person of the Trinity, shows us what radical *creatureliness* means. If we are to discover the end for which human beings have been created, if we are to know what it means to be human, we must look to the embodied Christ. And what we see there is a life lived in openness and obedience to God, Abba Father, and Creator. Such a life is characterized by giving to and for others. It is precisely in both his openness to the future and in his obedience to the Creator God who can be trusted that Jesus shows us embodied creatures what a realized, embodied human nature looks like. And there in the resurrection, ascension, and glorification of humanity in Christ, we see the reward of creaturely trust in God's benevolence.

In short, the doctrines of creation, incarnation, and resurrection provide a threefold divine valuation of materiality and embodiment. I contend that in them we have the resources to help us navigate the thicket of moral issues that present themselves at life's margins.

MORAL IMPLICATIONS: STEM CELLS, CLONES, AND OTHER REPRODUCTIVE TECHNOLOGIES

Before getting into specifics, let me first examine in a general way how the doctrines of creation, incarnation, and resurrection can guide us in thinking about stem cell research, human cloning, and other reproductive technologies. In the first place, the importance of *prenatal* life is underscored in the incarnation of Christ, whose bodily existence had its origins, like all mammalian life, as a fetus. The Second Person of the Trinity did not begin his embodied existence as a fully formed adult human being; rather, like us, he began his embodied existence *in utero*. His body developed from an astonishingly small, hollow sphere through an equally astonishing process of cell division and growth. During this process of cell division and growth, there came into being a fetus, the body of Christ. We Christians believe that that body existed on earth for roughly thirty-three years and then died before it was raised in a condition of glorification. The very doctrine of the incarnation of Christ, therefore, lends a *prima facie* high regard for prenatal life. I want now to tease out some specific implications of these doctrines for a more expansive ethic of life. But first, it will be helpful to explore the early stages of embryonic development. For it is important, I think, to get the biology right.

The Makings of a Baby

THE ZYGOTIC STAGE

From the fertilization of an oocyte (an egg) to the birth of a baby takes about thirty-eight weeks.[19] Fertilization begins when a sperm penetrates an oocyte (pronounced "oh-oh-site"), and it ends with the production of a short-lived, single-cell entity known as a zygote. The fertilization process takes roughly twenty-four hours. Between one and a half and three days after ovulation, the now fertilized egg, or zygote, begins to cleave or divide. This marks the end of the single-cell zygote.[20]

THE MORULA STAGE

After the first division, further divisions or cleavages occur roughly every twenty hours until a point is reached where there are sixteen cells. These sixteen cells are, like the aggregates that preceded them, contained within a translucid, spherical membrane called the zona pellucida. Because the aggregate of sixteen cells bears a striking resemblance to a mulberry, the developing embryo is called a morula

19. Probably the best reference guide to the makings of a baby is Keith Moore and Vid Persaud, *The Developing Human: Clinically Oriented Embryology*, 7th ed. (Philadelphia: Saunders Press, 2003).

20. Since the zygote is a single-cell object, as soon as division occurs and the number of cells multiplies, first into two and then into four and then into eight, the zygote ceases to exist. This is so for the plausible reason that one thing cannot be identical with many things. If we begin with a single thing and end up with two things, then either the original is identical with one of the two things or neither of them. Again, this is because one thing cannot be identical with two things (or four things or eight things). Since, in the case of cell division, there is no principled reason for identifying a zygote with one rather than the other cells after the first division, it is best to regard the zygote as having ceased to exist and to have been replaced by two new cells.

(from the Latin *morus*, or mulberry). All of these stages, and those preceding them, are preimplantation stages of embryonic development, meaning the stages take place before the developing embryo implants itself in the uterus, which usually begins between five to six days after fertilization and is completed between seven and twelve days after fertilization.

INDIVIDUAL OR COLLECTION?

Given the identity conditions for organisms offered in the last chapter, it is plausible to believe that from fertilization up through and including all of the preimplantation stages of the developing embryo (and even including some of the post-implant stages), an individual human animal or organism does not yet exist. Rather, what exists is a plurality or aggregate of cells (with the exception of the zygote, which is a short-lived, single-cell entity). The pertinent and extremely important philosophical question to raise here is this: *When does a collection or aggregate of cells compose an individual organism or living animal over and above the collection?* In other words, not all aggregates or collections of cells compose a human animal. Some compose a heart, and others compose an eye, and still others do not compose anything. The question, again, is this: When does a collection of cells compose an organism or animal? The answer suggested in the last chapter is this: *when those cells are caught up in a life.* More specifically, an organism exists when the highly coordinated activities of the cells are directed toward the maintenance of a stable, individuated, self-directing, self-maintaining, and homeodynamic event known as life.

It is reasonable to believe that the activities of the cells present during the early stages of embryonic development do not satisfy the identity conditions for an animal. Therefore, although the activities of the cells during the preimplantation stages of embryonic development are essential to the human organism or animal that will eventually develop, it is reasonable to believe that they do not themselves compose an organism or animal. When *do* the cells that make up the morula come to compose an individual organism? To answer that question, we must first chronicle some of the remaining stages of early embryonic development.

THE BLASTOCYST STAGE

After the morula stage comes the blastocyst stage of development, during which a fluid-filled cavity develops within the zona pellucida, and the sixteen cells within are replaced with others by way of continued cellular division. Therefore, strictly speaking, the collection of sixteen cells that developmental biologists refer to as the morula never composes an organism. Rather, the offspring of these cells—the cells that result from their division—or, more correctly, their offspring's offspring several generations removed come to compose an organism. In any case, during this stage of embryonic development, the zona pellucida disintegrates and the "hatched" blastocyst (the tightly compacted ball of cleaving cells) begins a process of rapid growth and implantation in the uterus. Implantation is usually complete by the end of the second week after fertilization.

To give you an idea of the size of the implanted blastocyst, it is approximately the size of the period at the end of this sentence. However minute, an awful lot of activity takes place in the area occupied by that minute ball of cells that is essential to the development of the fetus. Moreover, if monozygotic twinning is to occur (i.e., twins that develop from a single zygote as opposed to twins that develop from *two* zygotes—dizygotic twinning), it usually occurs during this stage.[21] This is important because it underscores something noted earlier. The zygote, I said, ceases to exist during its initial cleavage. This is because one thing cannot be identical with two things, and after the zygote divides, there are two cells. Since there is no principled reason for identifying the previously existing zygote with one or the other of the two cells that emerge after the first division, it is plausible to believe that the zygote—a single-celled entity—ceases to exist upon division. Similarly, as long as there is the possibility of an *aggregate* of cells dividing, there is reason to believe that the aggregate does not yet compose an organism over and above the aggregate itself. Consider: it is much easier to divide a *collection* of bottle caps than to divide a *single* bottle cap. The fact that division or twinning is possible for the collection of cells known as the blastocyst suggests that the aggregate does not yet compose a single living thing over and above the aggregate. So it seems to me that for as long as the possibility of twinning exists there is not yet a *single* living thing that the aggregate of cells composes.

21. Sixty-five percent of monozygotic twinning occurs during this stage, whereas approximately 35 percent of monozygotic twinning occurs within the first three days of fertilization. See Moore and Persaud, *Developing Human*, 148.

THE GASTRULATION STAGE

The third week after fertilization marks the beginning of the next stage of development, the gastrulation stage. Gastrulation is the beginning of what biologists refer to as morphogenesis (the development of body form). This is an incredibly important stage of development as the production of germ layers (i.e., ectoderm, mesoderm, and endoderm) during this stage gives rise to specific tissues and organs. Although the tightly compacted ball of cells (the blastula) is replaced through continued development, with an aggregate of cells of changing shape, we still do not yet have what developmental biologists refer to as a fetus. At the gastrula stage, however, a more important question for us than whether the aggregate of cells known as the gastrula composes a fetus is this question: Does the aggregate of cells known as the gastrula compose an organism? My honest answer is this: I don't know. What I do feel confident in saying is that clearly an organism is present during the *next* phase of development, the differentiation stage known as the organogentic period (weeks four through eight), during which tissues and organs are formed that are capable of performing specialized functions and during which the central nervous system is formed (between twenty-three to twenty-five days after fertilization). By the time a central nervous system is present and functioning, the activities of the aggregate of cells are clearly sufficiently highly coordinated and caught up in the maintenance of a singular life.

So, exactly when does a human organism come into existence? The best I think we can do is to point to an interval of time and not to a specific instant. Again, it seems at least that a human organism does not come into existence before the gastrulation stage (thirteen days after fertilization) or after the early organogentic period (twenty-six days after fertilization). Rather, sometime between the thirteenth and the twenty-fifth day after fertilization of the oocyte, the cells composing what biologists call the embryo are caught up in a stable, well-individuated, self-directing, and homeodynamic event (a life) and so compose an individual human organism.

It is interesting to note here that if this is correct, then a human organism exists *before* there is what developmental biologists refer to as a fetus. For the fetal stage of embryonic development does not commence until week nine, or fifty-six days after fertilization.

Preliminary Conclusions

The first thing to point out when considering the ethics of such things as embryonic stem cell research is that if what I say about developmental biology and the metaphysics of developmental biology is correct, it does not follow that it is morally permissible to do whatever we like to a blastocyst or a gastrula just because they are aggregates or collections of cells and not individual human organisms. Recall that if it is the case that an early term fetus is not a person, it does not follow that it is morally permissible to terminate the fetus's life. Likewise, just because a blastocyst is a highly compact ball of cleaving cells and not an individual organism, it does not follow that we have no obligations with respect to how we treat the blastocyst. Works of art or mountain ranges aren't living organisms, and it is plausible to believe that we have moral obligations with respect to how we treat them. On the other hand, it is also true that whatever obligations we might have to a blastocyst, a gastrula, and so on, those obligations are not as weighty as the obligations we have to a human person.

Moreover, the fact that we do not know exactly when between the thirteenth and the twenty-fifth day after fertilization a human organism comes to exist in the uterus does not create devastating difficulties either. If anything, it should produce in us an enormous amount of caution with respect to our manipulation of the contents of the uterus during this interval. Suppose, for example, that all you are told about a box is that it *might* contain a puppy. The mere *possibility* that it contains a puppy ought to move you to handle the box with care so as not to not cause injury in the event there *is* a puppy in the box. The fact that there *might* be a living, human organism in the womb thirteen days after fertilization ought to move us to treat the contents of the uterus with care on that day, and the next, and so on.

Stem Cells, Cloning, Reproductive Technologies, and the Creation-Incarnation-Resurrection Motif

With respect to the issues of human cloning, stem cell research, and other reproductive technologies, let's begin by distinguishing between cloning and stem cell research, since the two are, understandably, often confused. Let us take human cloning to be the asexual production of human beings who are virtual genetic duplicates of already existing individuals. As far as we know, the cloning of a human being has never been accomplished. I'll elaborate more on this in a bit. Stem cell research, on the other hand, sometimes involves cloning blastocysts for the purposes of gathering information and doing general science and for the purpose of what we might call transplant therapies. The idea involved in *embryonic* stem cell research is to remove embryonic cells that have not yet differentiated into muscle cells or nerve cells or pancreatic cells and the like and to place these as yet undifferentiated cells in cultures that, through human manipulation, will eventuate in the growth of the specific kind of cells needed. These grown and functioning cells can then be transplanted into patients to treat some defect or another.

We must keep in mind that embryos are not the only source of stem cells, though they are the only source of what developmental biologists refer to as *pluripotent* cells (cells that are virtually wide open with respect to what kind of cells they can become). Other sources of stem cells include adult blood cells, bone marrow, and umbilical cords. This is important to understand because when listening to many people discuss the issue of stem cell research, both in the media and in the public square, one might mistakenly come to believe that stem cell research refers merely to *embryonic* stem cell research. But that is simply false. Other sources of stem cells have been used for research, including stem cells obtained from mice, and such research has been going on for decades with not so much as a whisper of controversy. And it is not, as a matter of fact, implausible to believe that in the not-too-distant future technology will be available such that scientists will be able to produce embryonic-like stem cells (genetically duplicate cells [pluripotent cells] of you or me), without even the need of a blastocyst and therefore without the need of an embryo. We will come back to this shortly.

Embryonic Stem Cells

Before we get to some of the special ethical issues surrounding stem cell research and the like, let us get clear on what is so special about *embryonic* stem cells. As I have suggested, probably what makes embryonic stem cells so unique are the following features. First, they are self-replicating (they can produce more cells like themselves). Second, they have the capacity to differentiate into nearly every cell type that is present in a human organism (e.g., neurons, heart muscle cells, pancreatic cells, etc.). It is this feature of the cells that developmental biologists refer to as their pluripotency. Third, embryonic stem cells can differentiate outside a womb in a dish.

How are embryonic stem cells obtained, and how, exactly, are they used? This is where we confront the ethical issues head-on. The two most common ways of obtaining human embryonic stem cells are through surplus invitro-fertilized (IVF) embryos (eggs that are not fertilized *in utero* but rather at clinics dedicated to fertilizing and preserving the resultant embryos) and through cloning. In the latter case, an embryo is created by fusing a denucleated egg (cell) with a patient's own cell. The manufactured embryo is allowed to grow, and stem cells are then harvested from it. Because these cells are obtained from a clone, they are genetically compatible with the patient whose cell was fused with the denucleated egg. In the former case, stem cells are isolated by transferring the inner cell mass of a blastocyst into a dish that contains the requisite nutrients to promote the division and spreading of the cells contained in the inner cell mass. Soon (several days later) the cells proliferate and begin to fill the culture dish. The cells are then divided into several additional culture dishes. These cells then multiply, and the process of dividing them up and placing them in yet more culture dishes is repeated. The process is repeated over and over again for months. At about six months, the original thirty cells have proliferated into the millions. Cells that have multiplied over the course of six or so months and have not differentiated into any specialized cell type are regarded as pluripotent and are baptized an embryonic stem cell line.

We all know, of course, that the class of legal actions or activities and the class of moral actions or activities do not completely overlap. Some actions are legal that a person may find immoral (e.g., strip clubs, smoking, or abortions of human fetuses). Likewise, some actions or activities are not immoral but, in some states, are illegal (e.g., driving seventy miles per hour in an automobile). Whatever the legal status of harvesting human embryonic stem cells from spare IVF embryos, the practice ought to be considered morally serious from the perspective of the threefold theological motif of creation-incarnation-resurrection. Likewise, the practice of creating embryos through fusing a denucleated egg with a patient's own cell (for the purpose of extracting stem cells) is, from the perspective of our threefold theological motif, freighted with moral seriousness. The latter practice, it seems to me, is morally impermissible. The former practice, I believe, can be morally permissible.

Before I say why, let me say this. Though permissible, it would be, all things considered, morally better if we were not in the predicament we are in of having spare embryos. Indeed, we are currently faced with profound ethical conundrums concerning stem cell removal primarily because human embryonic stem cell production and cultivation involves a human embryo. More specifically, it involves the *destruction* of a human embryo. But current research indicates that the future of embryonic stem cell production may not involve embryos at all. Recall that one of the features that make human embryonic stem cells so special is their property of pluripotency, the ability of these cells to differentiate into virtually any cell type. Recent evidence suggests that *any* human cell can be massaged into pluripotency.[22] Therefore, it may soon be possible to obtain human embryonic-like stem cells (cells with all the relevant properties of human embryonic stem cells) without the need to create or destroy human embryos. If such a technique is ever fully developed, it will eliminate one major source of moral difficulties associated with human embryonic stem cell research.

The Ethics of Creating Excess Embryos

I want to make it clear from the outset that, so far as I can see, morally responsible parents ought to permit the creation only of embryos that they themselves intend for implantation and continued nurture. Similarly, IVF clinics, for their part, ought to create only embryos they intend to implant. Granted, not every attempt at implantation succeeds. However, the creation of more embryos than are intended for implantation seems morally problematic, as does the creation of embryos for the purpose of research. This is because, as we have learned, built into the doctrine of creation are the notions of *gift*, *creaturely dependence*, and *vocation*. Creation, including human beings, is a product of divine love, of divine giving. Part of human vocation consists in our call to acknowledge our dependence on God, the good Creator, and to respond in gratitude, trust, and obedience. Human creation or reproduction ought itself to mirror the divine giving of creation. To create human embryos without the intention to preserve, care for, and eventually place them in an environment

---

22. See Davor Soter, "New Paths to Human ES Cells?" in *Nature Biotechnology* 21 (October 2003): 1154–55. See also J. A. Byrne, S. Simonsson, P. S. Western, and J. B. Gurdon, "Nuclei of Adult Mammalian Somatic Cells Are Directly Reprogrammed to *oct*-4 Stem Cell Gene Expression by Amphibian Oocytes," *Current Biology* 13 (2003): 1206–13.

hospitable to life is to miscarry our human vocation. Reproduction is intrinsically a kind of giving and should not be transformed into a kind of taking. Creating a human embryo with the intention of disaggregating it or otherwise destroying it is surely not to mirror the divine giving. Therefore, deliberately creating more embryos than are intended for implantation, as well as cloning blastocysts with the intention of disaggregating them, is morally impermissible.

Is it *ever* morally permissible to create more embryos than are intended for implantation? Again, I think the answer has to be no. However, since there is a reasonably high probability that initial attempts at implantation will not succeed, the creation of multiple embryos does seem permissible. What follows ethically, it seems to me, is that couples ought to commit to implanting *exactly* the number of embryos created. Therefore, it is difficult to imagine a moral justification for creating more than three or four embryos at a time. And again, each embryo created should be implanted. If a couple consents to the creation of three embryos, then the couple ought also to consent to the implantation of all three. It follows, of course, that parents participating in IVF treatment ought to understand the likelihood and ramifications of carrying either twins, triplets, or quadruplets, depending on the number of embryos they agree to create. Thus, in an ideal world, there simply would not be the moral conundrum of what to do with spare embryos.

Moreover, the incarnation motif is also relevant here. It is important to keep in mind that the incarnate Christ is both the beginning of creation (Col. 1:15) and, at the same time, *rightful heir* to creation insofar as all things were created through him and for him. "All things" include human embryos in IVF clinics. These belong to God in Christ. They are not, ultimately, ours to do with as we please. This is why to create a human embryo without the intention of implanting it, or with the intention of instrumentalizing it (treating it as a mere object for scientific research), is to fail to realize its place in the divine economy of creation.

Our Obligations to Spare Embryos and the Question of Personhood

As I mentioned a moment ago, in an ideal world, the question of obligations regarding spare embryos would not arise. Unfortunately, we do not live in an ideal world. The real world is messy. The fact of the matter is that currently there are spare embryos. What are our obligations to them? Here, too, we must be guided by a theological commitment to embodiment as affirmed and reaffirmed in the interconnected doctrines of creation, incarnation, and resurrection. We must also keep in mind that, if what was said earlier about the biology of embryonic development is true, the embryos in IVF clinics are *not* human persons or even individual human organisms—they are blastocysts (aggregates of cells that do not compose a single human organism over and above the collection). That does not imply that we have no moral responsibilities or obligations with respect to them, but it ought to guard against our conceiving of the embryos as tiny persons.

Now some argue that a human embryo, from the moment of conception, *is* a person and therefore is endowed with the same rights as you or I. Those who hold such a view typically do so because the DNA present from the moment of conception contains all the directions for how the embryo will subsequently develop. Since the future unfolding of the developing embryo is set by the DNA, the embryo counts as a person.

As we have seen, I do not believe embryos are persons from the moment of conception. Indeed, I do not believe that we have a single human animal in the womb immediately upon conception. Moreover, and more importantly, it is a mistake to reduce personhood to information, which is precisely what a strand of DNA contains. Therefore, I find the reasoning employed for identifying newly conceived embryos as persons to be guilty of a kind of reductionism, reducing human personhood to information.

Some may object to the claim that a strand of DNA is "nothing but" information. That claim, it might be argued, is itself reductionistic and even false, for one might claim that a strand of DNA is actually a locus of potentialities. It should be noted, however, that a strand of DNA is nothing more than a strand of information; it is, if you will, a ticker tape code of uninterpreted symbols. Is that reductionistic? Yes, I guess it is. But we must bear in mind that some reductions are true. For example, lightning really is nothing but electrical discharge, and heat really is nothing more than mean, molecular kinetic energy. Therefore, rejecting reductionism with respect to persons or consciousness is not to reject all manner of reductions. Moreover, it is worth noting that a strand of DNA itself possesses no potentialities. An organism (or cell), however, may possess various potentialities in virtue of its DNA. But it is wrong to attribute the potentialities to the strand of DNA just as it is wrong to attribute to your ATM card the potentiality to deliver twenty dollar bills. The card is an information carrier. In the right environment (an ATM), the information on the card instructs something else (the machine) to spit out twenty dollar bills. DNA is like that. In the right environment (a cell or organism), it instructs the cell or organism to carry out particular functions (e.g., to make certain proteins).

One may object further along the following lines. Granted, a strand of DNA is nothing but information, but it is the embryo *with* DNA that is the relevant object of moral consideration here. And it, one might argue, is a person from the moment of conception since, given its DNA, all it needs is a hospitable environment in order to unfold all its potentialities according to the directions provided by its DNA.

My response here is twofold. First, as I have argued, from the moment of conception through to the twelfth or thirteenth day following conception, there is no single "it," no organism over and above the plurality of cells present (each containing DNA) that those cells jointly compose. In other words, no single organism, let alone a person, exists in the womb just after conception. Second, if the aggregate of cells just after conception is a person because of the presence of DNA, why is there just one person? Why not four, eight, or sixteen persons, since that is how many cells are present during different stages of cell division? And how about sperm with DNA, all by themselves, prior to conception? Each sperm has the potential to unite with an egg and, if placed in a hospitable environment and left to nature, would develop into a whole human being. Are there, in the vicinity of every adult male, millions of persons in the form of millions of individual sperm? Or how about female eggs all by themselves prior to conception? Are there as many persons as there are eggs? Each has the potential, if placed in the right environment (joined to a sperm and placed *in utero*) to develop into a whole human being. Thus, the argument for the personhood of an embryo based on the presence of DNA is fraught with difficulties.

Back to the Problem: Our Obligations to Spare Embryos

We are still left with the issue of what to do with spare embryos, embryos that remain after IVF treatments. Before addressing our obligations to spare embryos, let us set clearly before us just what the removal of stem cells means for embryos. First, we must keep in mind that the extraction from an embryo of *all* its stem cells results in the destruction of the embryo. However, it does not seem that the extraction of *some* of the stem cells should thereby destroy it. After all, some embryos at or before the blastocyst stage undergo twinning without destruction. On the other hand, and practically speaking, extracting *any* stem cells from a blastocyst exposes the embryo to great risk for destruction. In fact, I am not certain that extraction of only *some* human embryonic stem cells from embryos has ever been attempted. If it were attempted, I am told, it would come with high failure rates (high rates of destruction of the embryo because the technology is still at an experimental stage). We must be honest about the risks to the embryo, and we must also keep in mind that even if partial extractions were successful, the demise of the surviving embryo is practically guaranteed.

Given the risks, we must frankly ask how parents could possibly justify consenting to have stem cells removed from spare embryos, as I suggested earlier. Although the views I have been developing entail that the embryo is not a person (or even an organism), there is an analogy with persons that is helpful here. One can imagine the parents of a dying child justifiably consenting to have some of the child's cells, organs, or tissues removed for the benefit of others. Likewise, it can be morally permissible to donate the embryonic stem cells from surplus IVF embryos if doing so is directed toward the good of others and certain circumstances are present. For example, imagine a couple who has undergone IVF and has created three embryos, which they intend to implant. Now suppose that on the way to the hospital to have the embryos implanted the couple is involved in a tragic automobile accident that kills the mother, leaving behind in the clinic three embryos. Or imagine that it is discovered between the creation of the embryos and the implantation that implanting all three embryos would present a grave danger to the mother's health. Here are two kinds of situations that result in spare embryos even though the intention to implant all of them was satisfied. I believe that under these circumstances, the parents (or the surviving parent) may legitimately consent to stem cell removal for the good of others.

Some may argue that perpetual freezing is the preferred alternative in all cases of spare embryos insofar as perpetual freezing is the only alternative that recognizes the intrinsic worth of the embryos. While I understand and value the high regard for human life that leads some to hold such a view, I cannot support the view. Granted, perpetual freezing keeps the embryos in a kind of suspended animation and therefore keeps them in existence, but the view strikes me as committing the same sort of error as the view of those who support cryogenics (the perpetual freezing of fresh corpses in the hope that, eventually, technology will advance and make possible revivification). We Christians are surely called to value earthly life and to seek to preserve it, but not at any and all costs. Indeed, some things are worse than death. Suppose, for example, that your choices were to exist perpetually and consciously in the current fallen state of creation (perhaps in excruciating pain), to exist perpetually and unconsciously by being frozen under current fallen conditions, or to die a normal death. The choice to die a normal death seems preferable to the other alternatives. If the three alternatives for an embryo created with the intention to be implanted are perpetual freezing, discarding, or stem cell removal, perhaps stem cell removal is sometimes a morally permissible alternative.

A Qualified Endorsement of Embryonic Stem Cell Research

I believe we have reached a place in the discussion from which it is a bit easier to consider the great value of stem cell research and just how it can be construed positively through the trifocal lens of creation-incarnation-resurrection. The need for transplantable organs and tissues currently far exceeds supply. Stem cells, which can be coaxed and massaged to develop into specific cell types, open a path of hope for people who suffer with such things as Parkinson's disease, Alzheimer's disease, spinal cord injuries, burns, heart disease, diabetes, and the like. The hope lies in eventually providing a renewable supply of healthy tissues or muscles through the use of stem cells. Scientific research and technological development are not there yet. But the *potential* for development is promising.

Why is it easy to view such research and development positively through the threefold motif of creation-incarnation-resurrection? Because while recognizing the temptation for transplant therapies to become another Babel and also recognizing the fact that we ought not to hope for human immortality by way of technological achievement, we must at the same time recognize our call to anticipate the coming consummated kingdom of God. That kingdom is an *embodied* kingdom, and its citizens are whole and flourishing. As an eschatological people, a people who live their lives with this end in view (i.e., the consummated kingdom of God), we are called to establish small parables of that kingdom under current, fallen conditions. Working to heal God's image bearers from Parkinson's or Alzheimer's disease, not at any and all cost but responsibly and humbly, is a task that I believe *can* and *must* be embraced by Christ's followers. It is arguable that stem cell research and technological development of stem cell therapies fit within that calling.

Let me emphasize that there are dangers associated with even a very qualified endorsement of stem cell research, and we must make certain that we do not unwittingly succumb to them. The language used in popular debate over genetic and reproductive technologies reveals a disturbing societal trend from which the Christian community is not immune. I speak here of the tendency in our culture toward egoism, consumerism, and control, three vices at explicit cross purposes with the virtues that ought to characterize the people of God. For example, human cloning enables us to determine the very identity of our children. Through reproductive technology, human beings could now literally become projects of our own making (not begetting). Indeed, self-cloning reveals the almost unimaginable depth of egoist and narcissistic self-concern. Human cloning has the power to transform procreation into human "manufacture" and "commodification" (the production of human beings as artifacts or objects whose very existence owes to the design intentions of their producers). As a people of the kingdom, we must be vigilant in our stand against egoism, consumerism (of all kinds and on all levels), and control.

This is why I believe it is essential that we, as citizens of the kingdom of God, introduce into current discussions of these issues the truth that we human beings are social, *embodied* beings and what it means for us *as such* to bring forth new life. Recognizing our embodied nature, and recognizing the fact that creation is a gift to steward, can provide a necessary corrective to an overweening confidence in technology and an overly developed interest in the control of nature, including human nature through technology. But the potential benefits of embryonic stem cell research also fit into our calling to anticipate God's coming kingdom. It would be a mistake to lump embryonic stem cell research together with human cloning and in rejecting the one to reject wholesale the other. It seems to me, for the reasons suggested, that creating human embryos for the purposes of research or disaggregation is morally wrong, whether those embryos are created via

IVF technology or through fusing a denucleated egg with a patient's cell. But should technology make it possible to produce embryonic-like stem cells without the need to create or destroy human embryos, there are grounds for thinking that such a practice is morally permissible and perhaps even morally required of us. And again, it seems too that parents could justifiably consent to the removal of stem cells from spare embryos if certain conditions are met.

Preimplantation Genetic Diagnosis: Control or Stewardship?

One final reproductive technology remains to be considered: preimplantation genetic diagnosis (PGD). PGD makes it possible for parents at high genetic risk for such things as Tay Sachs, cystic fibrosis, sickle cell, and spinal muscular dystrophy to commence their pregnancy knowing that their offspring will *not* have these inherited and horrendous diseases. The process involves using the latest technology of molecular biology to locate and safely remove a single cell from three-to-four-day-old embryos that have been produced using the technology of *in vitro* fertilization. The process allows doctors to test the cells for the presence of a deadly disease, which the embryos have a high likelihood of carrying. By examining a cell from each embryo, the doctors can identify which embryos in the collection are *not* infected with the disease. This is done by identifying which of the cells fails to test positive for the disease. The embryos that do not carry the disease are then transferred to the womb, and the infected embryos are discarded.

Since PGD has an obviously good outcome (children being born free from a deadly disease), one may wonder on what grounds moral worries might be raised. But the ethical concerns are close to the surface. As already noted, some argue that a human embryo, from the moment of conception, is a human person and therefore endowed with the same rights as you or I. They believe this because the DNA present from the moment of conception contains all the directions for how the embryo will subsequently develop. Again, it is a mistake to reduce personhood to information. To the extent that we should consider such a technique as PGD as morally impermissible, we ought not to do so on the grounds that the embryo is a person. On what grounds ought we to register moral worries about PGD?

First, there are two worries here. One is that the same technology used to detect and delete *diseased* embryos could be used to detect genetic traits for hair color, eye color, gender, height, and so on, and then those embryos that fail to contain the desired traits could be deleted and destroyed. This is a real concern insofar as it recognizes the potential misuse of the relevant technology. As a Christian community, a community whose orientation toward the world is shaped by the Christian story and the threefold theological motif of creation-incarnation-resurrection, we must condemn eugenics in the strongest possible terms.

Eugenics is the putative improvement of the human race by controlled breeding. And, sad to say, we swim in a culture infatuated with improvement, a culture with an insatiable desire for perfection. For instance, we send our kids to learn French at eighteen months of age, sign them up not just for tennis camp in the summer but for year-round tennis preparation (beginning at early ages), and treat ourselves with botox to eliminate signs of aging. Some of us may even be tempted, if technologically possible, to *ensure* that our offspring are the best tennis players, or the most beautiful models, or the smartest students. In short, we want *perfect* kids. As I will soon argue, however, the use of technology for such eugenic purposes threatens the very meaning of parent-child relations.

The second worry is this. Although there is an important difference between using PGD to detect traits for hair and eye color and using PGD to detect traits for deadly diseases, the fact remains that the use of the technology for ensuring that parents at high risk for producing offspring with terrible diseases can commence their pregnancy knowing that their offspring will not be infected involves destroying embryos that do carry the disease. And this is morally problematic, not because doing so, in my view, destroys a person. It is morally problematic because it threatens the very meaning of parent-child relations.

The Challenge Presented by All Reproductive Technologies

The challenge for us Christians is to articulate a coherent view of what it means to be called to anticipate God's coming consummated kingdom of shalom—where all wounds are healed and all diseases defeated—by working to cure and eradicate diseases *while simultaneously* refusing to succumb to the eugenic impulses of our time. My own view is that we can succeed in articulating such a view. The challenge, however, is contained within the creation-incarnation-resurrection motif itself. For contained within the doctrine of creation is the notion of *gift*. And the notion of gift carries with it the idea of the given. My own particular embodiment—from my height to my hair and eye color, I did not choose; such characteristics were given. The same is true of our children. Our biological children are not *chosen* by us. They come to us as gifts, as given. They are not manufactured according to our prior specifications, like a piece of furniture specially built for us by a commissioned artisan. In fact, for some of us—some of the time—we may not have chosen our children if we did have a choice. It is the fact of their givenness, however, that underwrites our need to learn to love them as independent and imperfect creatures like ourselves. They are, in theological terms, *begotten*, not *made*.

The pressure from the other side comes from the incarnation and resurrection motifs, which have built into them, as suggested, the notions of restoration and future glorification. A restored, glorified human existence is an existence free from all defects that impoverish our human nature. Therefore, the question is how to hold simultaneously these two doctrines that seem at first blush to pull us in contrary directions—one toward acceptance and the other toward amelioration and change.

Struggling with the Tension

The doctrine of creation and the concomitant notion of gift and given ought to inspire in us a recognition *both* that we are not ultimately in control *and* that the destiny of the natural world does not belong to us but to divine action. The very fact of creation reminds us that we will not bring in the kingdom, effect our own immortality, or achieve a lasting restoration in this world of sorrows. At the same time, however, the doctrines of incarnation and resurrection remind us of our vocation to *anticipate* the coming *divinely established* kingdom of the new Jerusalem by establishing small parables or pictures of that kingdom. Supporting research and technological developments that aim at ameliorating and perhaps even curing terrible genetic defects can play a role in that anticipatory task. I believe that the tension between acceptance and amelioration, between the doctrines of creation and those of incarnation and resurrection, provides the very space within which we are to work out our salvation with fear and trembling. The doctrine of creation calls us to humility and trust, while the doctrines of incarnation and resurrection call us to scatter throughout this broken world examples of God's redeemed, restored, and reconciled creation, again, with fear and trembling. How should we apply this to reproductive technologies and PGD in particular?

While we must oppose any application of reproductive technology to eugenic tasks such as producing perfect children, we must, at the same time, I believe, support the responsible use of technology to the restorative task of curing disease. My objection, therefore, to using PGD to ensure that we do not produce children with a terrible disease is not that it destroys persons or even that it has an ignoble end. Rather, my objection is that it transforms reproduction and parent-child relations in ways that are at cross purposes with the doctrine of creation. It involves creating embryos with the intention of destroying those that do not meet our criteria for acceptance. It runs the risk of viewing children as commodities and looking to technology as our source of hope for a future where disease and sorrow are no more.

By the same token, if the production of embryonic-like stem cells is rendered possible without the need for either producing or destroying an embryo,[23] then we are right to support the responsible use of that technology for the restorative task of eliminating or curing disease. But when curing disease requires eliminating the *diseased*, something has gone terribly wrong.

Conclusion

We have covered quite a lot of ground in this chapter, so let's pull together the main threads of argument. In the first section I defended

23. Although technology has not yet made this possible, we are getting closer. See Irina Young Chong, Sandy Becker Klimanskaya, Joel Marh, Hi-Jiang Lu, Julie Johnson, Lorraine Meisner, and Robert Lanza, "Embryonic and Exrtraembryonic Stem Cell Lines Derived from Single Mouse Blastomeres," in *Nature* 439, no. 12 (January 2006). This article reports on a successful technique of obtaining stem cell lines (from mice) that does not involve the destruction of an embryo. The technique involves single-cell-embryo biopsy, a technique that does not hinder the developmental potential of the embryo. The authors seem to believe that if this technique would work on humans it would reduce or eliminate the ethical concerns associated with stem cell research. However, I am not as sanguine as they. It would surely eliminate one source of ethical difficulties, but not all, and perhaps not the more important issues associated with the morally appropriate applications or uses of stem cell lines. I suspect that if and when the technique is put to human use, we will be, morally speaking, in very much the same position with respect to it as we are with respect to preimplantation genetic diagnosis.

the Constitution View of persons against the charge that, as a materialist view of human nature, it has horrific ethical consequences. I argued that neither a metaphysics of materialism about persons nor a metaphysics of dualism about persons all by itself either entails or precludes an ethic of life. I pointed out too that, perhaps quite surprising, according to some versions of dualism, the abortion of a human fetus fails to destroy a human person, and, therefore, any prohibition against abortion based on such views cannot rely on the claim that abortions destroy persons.

In section 2 I developed the threefold theological motif of creation-incarnation-resurrection and pointed out the many ways in which these interconnected doctrines provide a profound valuation of embodiment and material existence. In section 3 I reflected on the difficult ethical issues surrounding stem cell research, cloning, and other reproductive technologies in light of the theological motif of creation-incarnation-resurrection. I argued that there are legitimate grounds for condoning embryonic stem cell removal from surplus IVF embryos but that the practice of creating embryos for the purpose of research or disaggregation must be condemned on the grounds that embryos are gifts over which we must exercise responsible stewardship. I suggested too that it may soon be technologically possible to produce embryonic-like stem cells without the need of embryos and therefore without the need to destroy embryos. Such a technological advance would remove one potent source of objection to stem cell production and associated therapies. I argued too that preimplantation genetic therapy is morally impermissible from the perspective of the doctrine of creation and that applying reproductive technologies toward the eugenic hopes of creating perfect children is to be condemned on the grounds that it conflicts with receiving children as gifts, a practice at cross purposes with manufacturing them as products. Finally, I pointed out how the tension presented by the doctrines of creation, incarnation, and resurrection is not to be resolved. Rather, such tension provides the space in which we are to work out our salvation with fear and trembling. The doctrine of creation calls us to humility and trust, while the doctrines of incarnation and resurrection call us to scatter throughout this broken world examples of God's redeemed, restored, and reconciled creation. Both tasks are ours to embrace with fear and trembling.

In the next chapter we turn to the issue of life after death and consider the challenge it presents to materialist views of human persons.

5

I Believe in the Resurrection of the Body and the Life of the World to Come

IN THE LAST CHAPTER WE considered some moral objections to the Constitution View of persons. I argued that CV does not have the ethical consequences it is alleged by some dualists to have and that, in fact, the emphasis on materiality is very much in sync with three key Christian doctrines: creation, incarnation, and resurrection. In this chapter I address another line of objection leveled against CV, namely, that materialist views of human persons like CV have a harder time accommodating the Christian hope of a future beyond the grave than does their rival dualism.

It is relatively easy to see the problem besetting a materialist view of human nature. The problem is simply this: It seems that bodies peter out and eventually cease to exist. And according to any plausible materialist account of persons, including CV, one's body is necessary for one's existence. Therefore, a constitutionalist, it seems, has quite a story to tell about how a body that peters out and ceases to exist can somehow turn up in the new Jerusalem. Or if a constitutionalist happens to believe in either an immediate resurrection or an intermediate state, then he or she has to tell some whopper of a story about how a body that has apparently died nevertheless continues to live. I say the story must be a whopper because often the corpse is right before our eyes. How then can a dead body be enjoying any kind of meaningful resurrection existence? Whatever the problems confronting dualism (and, as chapter 1 demonstrated, there *are* problems), it would seem that among them is not the problem of making sense out of the doctrine of postmortem existence.

This chapter consists of two parts. In the first part I show why it is plausible to believe that, contrary to appearances, Christian Dualists are no better off when it comes to making sense of the afterlife than their materialist siblings. For it is plausible to believe that a Christian Dualist, whether he or she realizes it or not, faces one of the same challenges as the constitutionalist: that of accounting for how a body that apparently falls apart and ceases to exist can nevertheless put in an appearance in the heavenly city. In the second part of this chapter I take up the challenge of providing just such an account. I begin with a presentation of the standard reassembly view of resurrection and suggest ways of defending that view against two common objections. I then reintroduce the plausible account of the persistence conditions for human bodies presented in chapter 3, an account that, at least on the face of it, seems to conflict with the reassembly view. I go on to offer reasons for believing that the account of the persistence conditions for human bodies is compatible with intermittent existence and also, therefore, with belief in the resurrection of the body, even if it should turn out that resurrection is not possible via reassembly. I close with a consideration of a non-gappy account of survival for friends of an intermediate state of conscious existence and those who embrace immediate resurrection. If I am correct in my diagnosis of Christian Dualists, namely, that they face one of the very same challenges as their constitutional brothers and sisters, then the discussion of resurrection that follows is important in its own right.

DUALISM AND LIFE AFTER DEATH

Recall Descartes's version of dualism. According to Descartes, properties can be divided into those that are mental (e.g., being in pain, desiring an ice-cream cone, or believing a proposition) and those that are physical (e.g., having a certain weight, shape, and mass). In chapter 1 we called this kind of dualism *Property Dualism*. Yet Cartesian Dualism adds to Property Dualism a claim about *substance*: A single thing can exist having properties of only *one* sort. This is what leads a Cartesian Dualist to claim not only that there *are* two fundamental kinds of substance but that there *must* be. Those two fundamental kinds of substance are un-extended, *thinking* substance (soul) and unthinking, *extended* substance (body). Descartes famously argued that he is essentially a thinking thing and therefore an immaterial (or unextended) soul or mind.

Remember too that, according to Descartes's view, my existence does not depend on my possessing either this or any other body. If Descartes is right, I could exist in a disembodied state. Descartes believed this because of the fundamentally dissimilar nature of souls and bodies. Since there is, for example, nothing in the nature of a soul that requires for its existence the existence of a body and nothing in the nature of a body that requires for its existence the existence of a soul or mind, Descartes reckoned that it is possible for the one kind of substance to exist without the other. And since Descartes was a Christian theist, he believed that it is *actually* the case that immaterial souls survive the death of the body.

In chapter 1 we saw how Emergent Dualism is not faced with the apparent problems presented by a decaying corpse. Since it is possible for God to maintain a soul in existence even after its gener-ating source (the human body) ceases to exist, there is no problem accounting for an afterlife.

I claimed, however, that it is plausible to believe that Christian Dualists have one of the same problems when it comes to postmortem survival as their constitutionalist siblings. We are now in a position to see why. While both Cartesian Dualism and Emergent Dualism are compatible with belief in an afterlife, neither William Hasker nor any Cartesian Dualist with whom I am familiar has offered an account of the Christian doctrine of the *resurrection* of the body. Yet it is plausible to believe that it is precisely that doctrine that needs to be addressed by Christian Dualists, for none of the ecumenical creeds of the church confesses belief in a doctrine of soul survival. The Christian doctrine has been understood as the doctrine of bodily *resurrection*. Contemporary dualists seem to have forgotten this in a way that our ancient dualist ancestors did not. Most if not all orthodox Christian theologians of the early church were anthropological dualists. It was these dualist-minded theologians who struggled in systematic ways to make sense of the Christian doctrine of bodily resurrection.[1] Telling a

1. For fascinating reading on the importance of bodily continuity and numerical sameness in patristic and medieval reflections on the resurrection, see Caroline Walker

story of how a body that apparently suffered a martyr's death can be numerically the same as a body that enjoys resurrection life is not the special preoccupation of twenty-first-century Christian materialists. This has been, at least until recently, a concern for dualists too.

You will recall that Thomas Aquinas believed that what accounts for the fact that a body once dead can nevertheless enjoy resurrection life is the fact that the human soul continues to exist, temporarily disembodied, between death and resurrection. That soul, Aquinas believed, organizes both the matter that composed the body before death and the matter that will compose the body after death. Same soul; therefore, same body.

As pointed out earlier, Aquinas's view of the soul is not without difficulties. What is relevant here is that unlike contemporary dualists Aquinas recognized the need to provide an account of the resurrection of the body. And like that of the dualists who preceded him, his view accounts for the *numerical sameness* of the resurrection and earthly body. In fact, it is plausible to believe that providing an account of the identity between the resurrected and the earthly body is constitutive of an account of the *resurrection* of the body, for the Christian doctrine is not the doctrine of reincarnation or the doctrine of the acquisition of some body or other any more than it is the doctrine of soul survival. Consider, for example, 1 Corinthians 15:42–43: "So will it be with the resurrection of the dead. The body that is sown is perishable, it is raised imperishable; it is sown in dishonor, it is raised in glory; it is sown in weakness, it is raised in power; it is sown a natural body, it is raised a spiritual body" (NIV). It is reasonable to believe that it is numerically the *same* body that exists before and after death, although after death that body is glorified and radically changed. For this reason, I think providing an account of the sameness of resurrected and earthly bodies ought to be of interest to *all* Christian philosophers, dualists no less than materialists.[2] Moreover,

---

Bynum, *The Resurrection of the Body in Western Christianity, 200–1336* (New York: Columbia University Press, 1995).

2. I say this in full recognition that it is, surprisingly, a minority view. Apparently, most contemporary philosophers of religion do not think the claim that the resurrection body is numerically the same as the premortem, earthly body is even plausible. See, for example, Bruce Reichenbach, *Is Man the Phoenix?* (Grand Rapids: Eerdmans, 1978): "The language of resurrection is misleading when it suggests that the very thing which died will be raised again. . . . [This] seem[s] generally contrary to any factual possibility, given the disintegration of bodies upon death and the dispersal of their constituent elements" (181). See also John Hick, *Death and Eternal Life* (New

given the fact that the Christian tradition has historically understood the doctrine of resurrection as involving numerically the same body, any putatively Christian view of the afterlife that departs from tradition at least owes an explanation for why we should understand the doctrine in a way that explicitly or implicitly departs from that tradition.

The Problem in Plain Terms

Just so we do not miss it, here is the problem that Christian philosophers face, both dualists and materialists. The apostle Paul died many, many years ago. If Paul's body, which existed in AD 45, exists in the hereafter, then a physical object numerically identical with Paul's body exists in the hereafter. But how could that be? There appear to be good reasons for denying that Paul's body could exist in the hereafter. Even if his body survived for some time as a fairly well-preserved corpse, the odds are that it has undergone radical decay over the years and has long since passed out of existence. How can a physical object that exists in the hereafter be numerically identical with a physical object that has either radically decayed or passed out of existence under more gruesome circumstances?

Note, it does not matter if you are an animalist who believes that Paul is *identical* with his body, a constitutionalist who believes that Paul is essentially constituted by his body (even if not identical with it), or a Cartesian Dualist who believes that Paul is an unextended, simple soul only contingently joined to his body. The questions apply to all. The following is my attempt to answer these questions.

Resurrection by Reassembly

There are two broad views of the resurrection of the body, and each is open to both materialists and dualists. There are gappy views of the resurrection and non-gappy views. In what follows I present

York: Harper & Row, 1976): "A human being is by nature mortal and subject to annihilation at death. But in fact God, by an act of sovereign power, either sometimes or always resurrects or reconstitutes or recreates him—not however as the identical physical organism that he was before death" (279). John Cooper, although he does not come right out and say it, seems to think that the resurrection bodies we human beings will enjoy in the afterlife are not the same numerical bodies we had in our pre-resurrection existence. See his *Body, Soul, and Life Everlasting* (Grand Rapids: Eerdmans, 1989), 185–95.

what I think are defensible versions of each, though I will end up endorsing a non-gappy version. Before I begin, however, I want to consider a common version of the gappy view that is not persuasive. This version is also historically the most dominant view of resurrection. According to it, resurrection is by reassembly.[3] The standard account of resurrection by reassembly secures the numerical sameness of the earthly and resurrected body, but even though some of the most popular objections against it can be met, it is still plausible to believe that the view suffers from a serious, if not fatal, flaw.

The reassembly view of resurrection is the view that our dualist ancestors seem to have favored. In this view, when God resurrects a human body, God gathers together all the smallest bits (the atoms) that compose a body at death, reassembles them, and causes them to be propertied and related in exactly the way they were propertied and related at the time of death. The resulting object, on this view, is the previously existing body. Before rejecting this view too quickly, we must frankly acknowledge that there are analogies to this view in common experience. For example, when a watch is taken in for repairs, thoroughly dismantled, cleaned, and later reassembled, what we are inclined to say is that the watch returned is numerically the same as the watch taken in for repairs. True, the watch did not persist through its disassembly and cleaning, but its constituent parts did. The watch received after repairs, according to this view, is the same as the watch taken in for repairs because it has all the same parts, and they are propertied and related in exactly the same way. According to the reassembly view of resurrection, the same is true with regard to human bodies.

There are, as I have mentioned, several objections to the standard reassembly view of resurrection. First, take this rather unpleasant example. Suppose your body becomes the tasty morsel of a cannibal, and some of the atoms that made up your body at death are also a part of the cannibal's body at death. How can God see to it that both you and the cannibal get reassembled, since now the very atoms in question have two equal claimants?[4] It would seem that God cannot resurrect both of you, since some of the atoms that composed your

3. See Bynum, *Resurrection of the Body in Western Christianity*, 27–42.
4. At issue is not cannibalism, as such, but the fact of part sharing. We could suppose that the atoms that compose a body at death eventually become part of the earth, which, in turn, become part of a chicken, which, in turn, become part of someone else's body at the time of his or her death. Same problem.

body at death composed the cannibal's body at death, and in order for God to resurrect either of you, God must reassemble *all* of the atoms that belonged to your respective bodies at death. So, the fact of atom sharing seems to tell against resurrection by reassembly. The defender of reassembly is not without a response to this objection. For atom sharing only prevents God from *simultaneously* resurrecting you and the cannibal. It does not prevent God from first resurrecting one of you and then, after the resurrected body has sloughed off the requisite atoms, using those same atoms to resurrect or reassemble the other body.[5] Atom sharing, therefore, does not preclude resurrection; it just makes it necessary that resurrection be temporally staggered.

Whatever the problems with a temporally staggered resurrection, there is also an additional problem. Consider once again the watch analogy. I suggested that gathering all the watch's parts and reassembling them—placing them in the same pre-cleaning relations to one another—would result in numerically the same watch. But there is a relevant disanalogy when it comes to the sorts of changes a human body can suffer without loss of identity and the sorts of changes a watch can suffer without loss of identity. For example, suppose you take your watch in for repairs and all or nearly all the parts of the watch are replaced. Surely the watch you receive after repairs is not the same as the watch you took in for repairs. The persistence conditions for watches, we might say, do not tolerate complete or nearly complete part replacement. Such is not the case, however, with human bodies. Human bodies are constantly sloughing off old bits and taking on new ones. In fact, the atoms that composed your body twenty years ago are not the same as the atoms that compose your body today.[6] And this presents a problem for the reassembly view of resurrection. One contemporary philosopher (Peter van Inwagen) puts it like this. Imagine that God were to take all the atoms that composed your body at age ten, and God reassembles them, placing the living human body that results right next to you. Who has your body, you or the reassembled ten-year-old? Or imagine that two thousand years from now God reassembles all the atoms that composed your body at the

5. My colleague Del Ratzsch pointed this out to me.
6. If you are inclined to object to this comparison on the grounds that the example of the watch was an all-at-once replacement of parts, whereas the replacement of atoms in humans occurs over time, I later offer reasons for thinking that a human being *can* survive (where a watch *cannot*) an all-at-once replacement of parts.

age of eighteen and also all the atoms that composed your body at the moment of your death at age ninety. Which is you? It would seem that either both are or neither is. Since you cannot be two things, it must be the case that neither is you.

What do these examples show? Well, they seem to indicate that *sameness of bits* is not among the persistence conditions for human bodies. In other words, while it is plausible to believe that gathering all the parts that composed your pre-repair watch and reassembling them will result in numerically the same watch, such is not the case with human bodies. Gathering all the atoms that composed your body at any stage of its past career and reassembling them will not result in numerically the same body.

If the defender of resurrection by reassembly were to insist that the atoms that composed the body at death are required for resurrection, we could ask, What is the principled reason for privileging *those* atoms? Why not the atoms that composed the body at age eighteen or age thirty? Why the atoms that composed the body at death?

A possible answer to these questions is suggested by the following examples. If you and I are watching a tennis match, and four sets into it the match must be postponed for a day because of rain, we would not consider the match that commences the next day as a *continuation* of the match we were watching a day earlier *if* when it commences it does so in the first game of the first set. But if the match commences where it left off the previous day, we would reckon it a continuation.[7] Likewise, with some artifacts. Take the watch. Even if all of a watch's parts that had been replaced over a ten-year period were recombined to compose a watch, we would not reckon the newly assembled watch numerically the same watch as that bought ten years ago. Why? Because many of us have the intuition that the parts composing a thing at its *last* moment, together with their properties and relations, are necessary for that object's reappearance. If a watch is dismantled and reassembled out of the parts that composed it at the time it was dismantled, those parts being propertied and related just as they were at the time of dismantling, then we would reckon the reassembled watch numerically the same watch. So when it comes to resurrection by reassembly, there is an intuition that explains why

7. For a defense along these lines, see David B. Hershenov, "The Metaphysical Problem of Intermittent Existence and the Possibility of Resurrection," *Faith and Philosophy* 20 (2003): 24–36.

we prefer the atoms that composed a body at death and *not* the ones that composed the body at age eighteen or age thirty.

Aside from particular worries peculiar to this line of response, it is the larger issue of the persistence conditions for bodies that leads me ultimately to reject the standard reassembly view of resurrection. Persistence conditions for things of a certain kind tell us what sorts of changes things of that kind can undergo without ceasing to exist. To use an earlier example, the persistence conditions for bananas are such that a banana can persist through color changes (the same banana can be green on Monday and yellow on Friday), but it cannot persist through changes that render it an ingredient in banana bread.

THE PERSISTENCE OF BODIES AND THE RESURRECTION

In chapter 3 I offered an account of the persistence conditions for human bodies. That account sets in sharp relief what I take to be the problem with the standard reassembly view of resurrection.

Causal considerations seem especially relevant to the persistence of material objects of any sort, and the kinds of causal dependencies relating an object at earlier and later stages of its career seem to differ according to the kind of object whose career we are tracing. Different kinds of persisting things have different persistence conditions. What it is in virtue of which a *human body* persists is different from what it is in virtue of which a *computer* persists. When it comes to the persistence of bodies, I suggested the following:

> If an organism O that exists some time in the future is the same as an organism P that exists now, then the (set of) simples that compose P now must be causally related to the (set of) simples that will compose O in the future.

I specified further that the relation must be of the *immanent* causal and life-preserving variety. I named this condition on the persistence of bodies the immanent causal condition, or ICC. I did so because the relevant causal relation takes place within a single object. In other words, a state x of thing A brings about a consequent state y in A itself, and not in a numerically distinct object, B. Earlier I put it this way:

A human body B that exists in the future is the same as a human body
A that exists now if the temporal stages leading up to B are immanent
causally connected to the temporal stage of A now.[8]

It should be pointed out that the immanent causal condition applies
during any temporal stretch during which we exist. If our existence
can have gaps in it (if we can exist, cease to exist, and then begin
again to exist, as I believe is possible), then, quite obviously, the
condition does not apply *during* the gap (during the temporal stretch
during which we do not exist). The condition is a condition for our
persistence or *continued* existence.

Some philosophers hold that it is impossible for a material thing
to have two beginnings (a material thing like an organism cannot
begin to exist, cease, and then begin again to exist). I am not among
those philosophers. I see no *a priori* reason to reject the possibility of
gappy existence. I admit, however, that absent a miracle, the prospects
for gappy existence look pretty bleak. But I am a Christian theist,
and I believe in miracles. Therefore, the reassembly view cannot be
rejected because it would involve a miracle. The problem with the
reassembly view must lie elsewhere.

Let us return to the issue of reassembly. The problem with the
standard reassembly view of resurrection is that it seems to conflict
with the immanent causal condition for the persistence of bodies.
While it is true, according to the standard reassembly view, that the
atoms in a resurrected body are the way they are because the atoms
in the body just before death were the way they were, it is not the
case that the two stages of the body's existence are *immanent* causally related. Instead, according to the standard reassembly view, the
causal chain runs through God. God reassembles the original bits
based on their arrangement at death. My concern with the standard
reassembly view of resurrection, then, is not that it requires gaps
in a thing's existence but that it fails to meet the immanent causal
requirement for the persistence of bodies.

It has been pointed out by Dean Zimmerman and Hud Hudson,
two Christian philosophers who hold radically different views about
human nature, that a certain kind of reassembly view may in fact be
compatible with the immanent causal requirement for persistence.

---

8. For more on the notion of immanent causation, see Dean Zimmerman, "Immanent Causation," *Philosophical Perspectives* 11 (1997): 433–71.

They point out that ICC rules out the need for a state or event that is present during the temporal gap during which the body is not present and is itself causally sufficient for the later stage of the body's existence. That requirement, however, would not be violated if God were to issue a decree of the following form, "Let there be a resurrected body that is composed of the same parts, propertied and related in just the same way as the parts that composed Paul's body at his death," which was then followed by the appearance of said body. God's decree, in other words, though causally *necessary* for the reappearance of Paul's body, is not causally *sufficient* for its appearance and therefore would not transgress the immanent causal requirement.[9]

While I agree that the divine decree or "back-tracking" version of the reassembly view could be made compatible with ICC, I would insist on the following: that the parts that compose the post-gap body are the way they are at least partly in virtue of the causal contribution of the pre-gap parts (and their properties and relations). If that condition is met, then such a reassembly view can succeed. However, I also think that there are aesthetic reasons for preferring a view of the resurrection that involves God on the front end of the gap, perhaps even at the beginning of creation, bestowing on the parts that compose bodies a capacity for passing on causal "umph" across temporal gaps and issuing a general decree, also at the beginning of creation, to the effect that when the requisite conditions obtain that capacity is exercised. Such a view would be preferable to any reassembly view according to which the mere presence of the parts of a body (and their properties and relations) at death are, together with God's decree, causally sufficient for the reappearance of the body after death (a la Zimmerman). So although the standard reassembly view of resurrection may be at odds with the immanent causal condition on the persistence of bodies, it is possible to construct an alternative that is not.

But let us suppose for the sake of argument that resurrection is *not* possible via reassembly. Would it be possible at all? It is reasonable for Christians to believe the answer is yes. But how? In answering this question, we will see why it is plausible for Christians to believe

9. Such a view has been suggested in Dean Zimmerman, "The Compatibility of Materialism and Survival: The Falling Elevator Model," *Faith and Philosophy* 16 (1999): 194–212; and Hud Hudson, who raised this when commenting on a paper I delivered at the 2002 Wheaton Philosophy Conference.

that resurrection is compatible with gappy existence even if, as we suppose, it is not possible via reassembly.

GOD AND THE GAP

Is it plausible to believe that *immanent* causal relations can cross a temporal gap? I think it is. Here is why. First, we know from revelation that God promises resurrection, and experience seems to teach us that bodies cease to exist. If it is true that a future body is going to be numerically the same body as one that previously existed but ceased, then what the account of persistence for bodies I have offered tells us is that the last stage of the pre-gap body and the first stage of the post-gap body must stand in immanent causal relations to each other. And this would require that immanent causal relations cross the temporal gap. But *can* they? As Christians, we have reason to think so. In fact, here is an argument to that conclusion.

1. Bodies cease to exist.
2. Scripture teaches that our bodies are going to be raised.
3. If a future body is going to be numerically the same body as one that previously existed but ceased, then the last stage of the pre-gap body and the first stage of the post-gap body must stand in immanent causal relations to each other.
4. Therefore, immanent causal relations can cross temporal gaps.

Assuming that a requirement for my body to exist after ceasing is that the two relevant stages of its existence (the last stage of the pre-gap body and the first stage of the post-gap body) be immanent causally related, it *must* be true that immanent causal relations can cross gaps. The challenge for Christians who embrace ICC (dualist or materialist) is to understand just how that might work. But regardless, insofar as one believes that the argument is sound, it provides one with good reason for believing that gappy existence is compatible with the controversial claim that immanent causal relations can cross temporal gaps.

I admit however, that I haven't a clue how this might work. The problem is that it is completely opaque to me how the atoms that compose the pre-gap body can pass on a life-preserving causal relation across the gap to the atoms that compose the post-gap body. So let us suppose, for the sake of argument, that it is not possible for this to happen. Does it follow that resurrection life is therefore impossible? Absolutely not! One could argue that ICC is a *diachronic* condition (it applies *across* time, connecting earlier and later stages of, in this case, a single organism). But take the first instant of my body's pre-gap existence. At that instant, there are no stages to be immanent causally connected. But it is *that* body that God causes to exist. Well, if God causes that body to exist once, why couldn't God cause it to exist a second time? Perhaps like the first time, once it is brought into existence, what will make it the case that a later stage is a stage of the same body is that immanent causal relations link those stages. But what makes the first stage of the post-gap body a different stage of the same body that perished is that God makes it so.

That is one thing that could be said, and I think it is an extremely plausible thing to say. But another thing that could be said is that if one insists that if any two stages are to be different stages of the same body, then those stages must be immanent causally connected, the "must" needn't be a *metaphysical* "must" (a "must" that applies in every possible situation). It could be a *nomological* "must" (it could be what must occur given the laws of nature that exist in the world we inhabit). In other words, one could argue that ICC is not a *metaphysically* necessary condition on the persistence of bodies but a *nomologically* necessary one. Since it is reasonable to believe that the natural laws that govern the postmortem world of the new Jerusalem will be quite different from those governing this world, it may not be the case that immanent causal connections unite the last stage of the pre-gap body and the first and succeeding stages of the post-gap body. Even so, all of those stages could be stages of the *same* body.

So I believe that the prospects for gappy existence are quite good. And for those who think gappy accounts sit ill at ease with the apparent teaching of Scripture that we do not cease to exist but continue to exist immediately upon death, gappy views do preserve another apparent teaching of the New Testament, namely, that death marks a tragic end to our existence. The New Testament clearly teaches that death is an enemy finally conquered in the resurrection of Jesus. So, if gappy existence does not sit comfortably with some parts of Scripture, it sits very comfortably with others.

NON-GAPPY SURVIVAL: FISSIONING OF CAUSAL PATHS

But let us suppose that you believe, as I am coming to believe, that Scripture and tradition teach immediate or non-gappy survival. Suppose, in fact, that you believe that a single thing cannot have two beginnings, that a thing cannot begin to exist, cease to exist, and then begin again to exist. (I do not believe this, however.) How can there be a body in heaven numerically the same as a body I watch die if there is no such thing as gappy existence?

In different places, Dean Zimmerman and I have argued that one answer to this question lies in the fissioning or splitting of causal paths. It seems possible that the causal paths traced by the simples caught up in the life of my body just before death can be made by God to fission, such that the simples composing my body then are causally related to two different, spatially segregated sets of simples.[10] One of the two sets of simples would immediately cease to constitute a life and come instead to compose a corpse, while the other would continue to constitute a body in heaven or wherever an intermediate state of existence is enjoyed.[11] In other words, the set of simples along one of the branching paths at the instant after fission fails to perpetuate a life, while the other set of simples along the other branch continues to perpetuate a life. If this is at least possible, as it seems, then a view of survival exists that is compatible with the claim that human bodies cannot enjoy gappy existence.

This view of immediate survival is compatible with both immediate resurrection and an intermediate state of conscious existence between death and resurrection. Like most other views in the neighborhood, however, it does not come without a price. At least part of the cost involves giving up the assumption that material continuity is necessary for the persistence of physical objects. Moreover, whereas we may be willing to allow physical organisms in particular gradually to replace some or all of the matter that constitutes them, we may not be willing to allow for an all-at-once replacement like that entailed by the fissioning

---

10. Dean Zimmerman was the first to suggest this view in a paper presented at the Pacific Division APA meeting in 1994. I take up the view in my "Persons and Bodies," *Faith and Philosophy* 15 (1998): 324–40. Zimmerman develops it further in his "Compatibility of Materialism and Survival," 194–212.

11. We will assume not only that persons are essentially persons but also that being alive or conscious is a necessary condition for human personhood. Therefore, after the fissioning there is only one possible candidate for a person-constituting object, since the surviving corpse is not a living organism and thus not capable of subserving consciousness.

of causal paths. We may think that is too high a price to pay. However, insofar as what ultimately matters for the persistence of organisms is the holding of immanent causal relations between any two stages of an organism's career, giving up the assumption about material continuity is not a cost incurred by the view but rather an entailment of it.

There is a more serious metaphysical problem with the fissioning of causal paths, however: It seems to violate what has come to be called "the only x and y" principle. According to this principle, whether some objects x and y compose some concrete individual F should have nothing to do with events involving numerically distinct objects spatiotemporally segregated from F. But in the account of immediate resurrection just suggested, it looks as though whether a body persists into the afterlife has everything to do with what happens to the other fission product, namely, that it immediately perish. I have answered this charge elsewhere in some detail and therefore will not take it up here,[12] except to say that there are good reasons for believing that it can never be the case that a competitor for identity with my body can exist.

CONCLUSION

When I talk to Christian Dualists about the afterlife, I am frequently met with something like the following response: "Wow, am I ever glad I'm a dualist! I mean, whatever the problems with dualism, at least we don't need any wacked-out metaphysical prestidigitation to make sense of postmortem survival." If the issue is simply one of postmortem survival, then I admit that dualists have a much easier time accommodating such a doctrine. But if one is both a dualist and a *Christian*, then it is plausible to believe that such an individual has at least one of the same problems as Christian materialists, namely, how to make sense of the Christian doctrine of the resurrection of the body. In this chapter I have suggested one way a Christian, dualist or materialist, might provide a non-gappy account of that doctrine and also offered reasons for believing that a gappy account of survival is compatible with a plausible condition on the persistence of human bodies.[13]

12. See my "Physical Persons and Post Mortem Survival without Temporal Gaps," in *Soul, Body, and Survival*, ed. Kevin Corcoran (Ithaca: Cornell University Press, 2001), 201–17.
13. I wish to thank the Tuesday afternoon philosophy colloquium at Calvin College and the following individuals, Rebecca DeYoung, Hud Hudson, Trenton Merricks, Christina Van Dyke, and Dean Zimmerman, for helpful comments on the content of this chapter.

6

The Constitution View and the Bible

SOME FINAL THOUGHTS

I WANT TO REITERATE HERE WHAT I said in the introduction; namely, whatever the truth about our nature, it is not transparent and obvious. Is dualism the truth about our nature? In chapter 1 I tried to explain why I don't find Substance Dualism, Compound Dualism, or Emergent Dualism ultimately persuasive. That, of course, is perfectly compatible with one of those views being true. But there seem to me good reasons for thinking that those views constitute false accounts of our nature, and in chapter 1 I attempted to say just why I think that's so.

Nevertheless, I do not for a moment regard Substance Dualism (or some of the other dualisms) as benighted, boneheaded, or otherwise less than intellectually respectable. I think, in fact, that Substance Dualism is correct in its assertion that we human persons are *not* numerically identical with human bodies. What I deny is that the only way this could be true is if we are identical with (or have as essential parts) immaterial souls, as dualism asserts. Moreover, dualist views of human nature are all too often discounted out of hand without so much as an argument. That is preposterous. Substance Dualism may be false, but it is assuredly not a nonstarter. And it is clearly compatible with important Christian commitments. So although in the end I reject a dualist picture of human nature, I do not for a moment think the view is silly, incomprehensible, or intellectually subpar.

In the second chapter I explained what people mean when they claim that we are identical with our bodies. As I indicated, there are at least two ways to understand the claim: that we are identical with an aggregate of atoms or cells and that we are identical with human animals. My aim was to say why I find both interpretations beset with insuperable difficulties. I said emphatically that we are *not* numerically identical with a collection of atoms, nor are we identical with human animals. Yet just as I think there is some truth to Substance Dualism—we are *not* identical with our bodies—so, I said, there is a sense in which it is true to say we *are* animals. The sense in which it is true to say we are animals is the sense in which it is true to say we are wholly physical objects *constituted by* (without being identical with) our animal bodies. There is no material part of me that is not also a part of the organism that constitutes me, and I have no immaterial parts. To concede this to animalism is not to concede that we are *identical with* animals. It is simply to say that, just as I believe Substance Dualism is false but contains an element of truth, so I believe animalism is false but contains an element of truth.

Chapter 3 consisted of my proposed alternative to animalism and dualism. Here I drew an analogy between dollar bills, diplomas, and dust jackets—and the things that constitute them—and human persons and the things that constitute them (human organisms). I argued that just as dollar bills, diplomas, and dust jackets are not numerically identical with the things that constitute them (they have different persistence conditions, histories, etc.), so human persons are not identical with the things that constitute them. Even so, just as dollar bills, diplomas, and dust jackets are wholly material objects, even if not the material objects that constitute them, so too are human persons wholly material objects, even if not identical to the material objects that constitute them. The Constitution View, I wanted to suggest, gives us a way to appropriate the insights of animalism (we *are* animals) and dualism (we are *not* our bodies) without giving in to the excesses of either (i.e., without embracing the claim that we are *identical with* our bodies and without embracing the claim that we are *identical with* immaterial souls).

In chapter 3 I also provided an account of the persistence conditions for human persons. I said that human persons are *essentially* constituted by their bodies (they cannot exist and fail to be constituted by their bodies) and also *essentially* psychological (they cannot exist and fail to possess the capacity for a first-person perspective). As I put it, a *necessary* condition for my continued existence is that my body persist, and what is both necessary and *sufficient* is that this body continue to subserve a capacity for first-person intentional states.

After turning back a battery of philosophical objections (and a couple of theological ones) to CV, I set my sights in chapter 4 on addressing the moral challenges presented by the view. Given CV as presented, it is possible for something to be human without also being a person. If that is true, then it appears we have no moral obligations to these human nonpersons. That, I said, is false. Just because something is not a person does not entail we have no moral obligations with respect to it. But I also stressed that a metaphysical view of human nature *all by itself*—be it dualist or materialist—neither entails nor precludes an ethic of life. I argued that there are other grounds for moral obligation than simply the personhood of an entity, including human but nonpersonal entities.

Then I turned to the Christian narrative to provide the needed resources for helping us think about difficult beginning of life moral issues. I showed how the doctrines of creation, incarnation, and resurrection provide a perspectival grid through which we can fruitfully think about the ethical issues surrounding embyronic stem cell research, human cloning, and other reproductive technologies. I pointed out how these theological motifs underwrite materiality and embodiment and how stem cell transplant therapies can be viewed in a positive light based on them. While I acknowledged an apparent dilemma—that the doctrine of creation seems to call us to accept diseased embryos and to reject the removal of cells from a three-day-old embryo—the doctrines of the incarnation and the resurrection seem to call us to ameliorate disease in an attempt to anticipate the new Jerusalem, where human beings will be glorified and restored. I suggested that there really is no irresolvable dilemma insofar as we are called *both* to humility and responsibility and to anticipate God's kingdom of wholeness and well-being. Here I offered a qualified endorsement of human embryonic stem cell research and suggested that in the future one line of objection (that extracting embryonic stem cells involves the creation and destruction of an embryo) may no longer apply, since it may be possible in the future to massage any human cell into pluripotency, the "magic" feature of human embryonic stem cells.

Finally, in the last chapter I tried to provide a coherent view of the afterlife on the assumption of a materialist metaphysic of persons. I argued that although resurrection requires a miracle, there is no reason to believe that the miracle cannot involve either gappy existence (we live, we die, and then after an interval during which we do not exist we are brought back into existence) or an intermediate state of conscious, embodied, but not yet glorified existence. The fact of the matter is this: Whether you are a dualist or a materialist about human persons, if you are a Christian, you need an account of the Christian doctrine of the resurrection of the body. Dualism does not excuse you from needing such an account. The accounts I offered have the ecumenical virtue of being neutral with respect to a dualist view of human nature and a materialist view.

THE CONSTITUTION VIEW AND THE BIBLE

Many readers are no doubt wondering how my proposed alternative to dualism, the Constitution View, coheres with the biblical materials. Let me make two general comments to begin. First, the Jewish and Christian Scriptures simply are not interested in the level of philosophical nuance that occupies philosophical accounts of human nature like this one. An anthropology that has a legitimate claim to being biblical emphasizes the relational or communal understanding of authentic human existence rather than getting bogged down in the details of *philosophical* or metaphysical analysis. Even so, if we want to ensure that a philosophical anthropology coheres with Scripture, we must present an account of what it means to be human that takes seriously the need for a fully embodied personhood that makes relationships with God, the human family, and God's creation possible. CV certainly succeeds on this score, even if the view is, quite self-consciously, a "philosophical" (as opposed to a "biblical") view of human nature. In other words, I have made no pretense to present a biblical view of human nature. What I have done is to offer a philosophical view of human nature that coheres with the biblical witness.

Second, if we are to appreciate the narrative structure of Christian Scripture, we cannot resolve philosophical questions on the basis of what a select number of proof texts say, as though the deciding factor at every turn is how we are able to address the question, But what about *this* text? By *Christian Scripture*, we mean the canon of Scripture, which comprises a grand narrative from creation to new creation. What this narrative entails about a portrait of the human person is far more significant than what any single text might say. Hence, the most important question is not, What does *this* text teach about the human person? but How should we understand this text *within the whole narrative of God's Word?* Indeed, biblical scholars have begun to address this very question and have done so in ways that demonstrate at least the plausibility, perhaps even a preference for, non-dualist readings of individual texts.[1] This may be surprising, however, since we so easily find dualism to be the obvious view of some important texts. But the fact that we so easily find dualism in the relevant texts may be because the (extra-biblical) narrative within which we have understood those texts is itself a dualist one.

Perhaps it will help to consider briefly what many regard as the biblical case for dualism.

A BIBLICAL CASE FOR DUALISM

The Old Testament

A typical line of argument for dualism based on the Bible goes like this. Since the Old and the New Testament teach an intermediate state of conscious existence between death and the general resurrection, soul-body dualism must be true. The idea is that if our bodies have ceased to exist but we continue to enjoy conscious experience, then the only way that is possible is if we are *not* identical with our bodies.[2] And the only way we can fail to be identical with our bodies is if we are immaterial souls or, as some put it, if we have a personal part, dimension, or aspect that can survive physical death.[3]

Notice that the argument is not that sacred Scripture *explicitly* teaches dualism. The argument is that Scripture appears to teach

---

1. See, for example, the following: Robert A. Di Vito, "Old Testament Anthropology and the Construction of Personal Identity," *CBQ* 61 (1999): 217–38; Philip Hefner, *The Human Factor: Evolution, Culture, and Religion* (Minneapolis: Fortress, 1993); Ted Peter, Robert John Russell, and Michael Welker, eds., *Resurrection: Theological and Scientific Assessments* (Grand Rapids: Eerdmans, 2002); and Christoph Schwöbel and Colin E. Gunton, eds., *Persons, Divine, and Human: King's College Essays in Theological Anthropology* (Edinburgh: T & T Clark, 1991).

2. See John Cooper, *Body, Soul, and Life Everlasting* (Grand Rapids: Eerdmans, 2003), for a fine example of this sort of argument.

3. Again, see ibid.

something that *implies* dualism, something that could not be true *unless* dualism were true. For example, consider Old Testament passages that admonish against consulting the dead (e.g., Lev. 19:31; 20:6; Deut. 18:11; Isa. 8), passages that one may believe do not make sense without the belief that the dead continue to exist in some conscious yet disembodied state. Then there are passages like those in 1 Samuel where a dead Samuel is summoned up from the grave by the witch of Endor and seen by Saul himself (1 Sam. 28). After considering these Old Testament passages and others dealing with the hope of resurrection (e.g., Ps. 16:10; Isa. 26:19; Ezek. 37; Dan. 12:2), John Cooper says this: "[The] conclusion is inescapable. Persons are not merely distinguishable from their earthly bodies, they are separable from them and can continue to exist without them. . . . The logic is just as inexorable. Dualism is entailed."[4]

There are several things to say in response to the case for dualism based on Old Testament interpretation. First, with respect to those Old Testament passages dealing with the hope of resurrection, I am familiar with two ways of interpreting these texts, and neither favors a dualist anthropology. Some interpret the texts as metaphors for Israel's return from exile, which, if true, have no real bearing on the debate concerning anthropology. The other way of interpreting the texts is the ordinary way, namely, as giving voice to the hope of a future and literal resurrection. Hope for resurrection, however, is hope for *bodily* existence beyond the grave and is not even suggestive of an intermediate state of *disembodied* conscious existence between death and future existence. As I argued in chapter 5, however, belief in the resurrection is eminently congenial to a materialist view of human nature.

More important, however, is the fact that none of the Old Testament passages frequently pointed to as implying disembodied conscious existence implies it at all. Take the witch of Endor passage, for example. Clearly, Samuel is experienced as some sort of *bodily* being. He is *seen*, after all. In other words, even if Scripture teaches an intermediate state of conscious existence (which I believe it does), it does not imply that the state is a *disembodied* state. An intermediate state of existence is compatible with a *bodily* state of existence. The intermediate-state bodies would not be the glorified bodies they will be in the new Jerusalem, but they would be such as are fit for

4. Ibid., 69.

subserving conscious life between death and the general resurrection. None of the relevant Scripture passages from the Old Testament rules out an intermediate state of conscious bodily existence.

I think we are led to construct the following piece of fallacious reasoning as a result of what the Old Testament says concerning life after death:

> If there is an intermediate state of conscious existence between death and the general resurrection, then human persons must be dualistic in the sense of having an immaterial soul.

But we must take care not to confuse the true claim that

> *if* human persons enjoy an intermediate state of conscious existence, then human persons are *not* identical with what gets buried in the earth,

with the false claim that

> *if* human persons enjoy an intermediate state of conscious existence, then human persons are immaterial souls.

I argued in chapter 3 that human persons can be essentially constituted by their bodies without being identical with them. Likewise, it is possible for there to be an intermediate state of conscious existence *without* a dualist anthropology. To put it sharply, human persons are not identical with their bodies but are nevertheless wholly material beings. Chapter 3 provided reasons for believing this puzzling claim. The important point here is simply to see that it is a mistake to move from what seems to me to be the true claim that the Old Testament teaches an intermediate state of conscious existence to the claim that we are therefore immaterial souls.

One may grant my logical point here and nevertheless argue that the strongest case for a dualist anthropology can be made not from Old Testament interpretation but rather by appeal to New Testament teaching. So let's look at the New Testament case for dualism.

The New Testament

Most orthodox Christians believe there is a period of time between death and the general resurrection during which they will reside with

Christ. And it may seem that if human beings are material beings, then an intermediate state is impossible.[5] It is a flat impossibility, one may think, because at death bodies cease to exist and therefore so too the person. As I have already suggested, this is fallacious insofar as it assumes that the corpse left behind is what a human person must be identical with if human persons are physical objects. So, there are two points to make here. First, as stated in chapter 3, it is a mistake to identify a body with a corpse. A corpse is a heap of matter that used to compose a body, and a body or organism is essentially living. A corpse is no more a body than a heap of bricks and mortar after an earthquake is a building. The second point is this. Not only is it a mistake to identify a corpse with a body, but it is also a mistake to identify a person with a body or organism. Indeed, in chapter 3 I showed how we human persons can be wholly physical and yet not identical with our bodies. In any event, and more to the point of the biblical case for dualism, there are two alternatives to belief in an intermediate state: belief in *immediate resurrection* and belief in a period of *nonexistence* and then at some future time *re-creation*.

John Cooper surveyed the New Testament to adjudicate among what he perceives as the three competing and exhaustive choices for what awaits us immediately after death. (1) We continue to exist by being immediately resurrected. (2) We continue to exist in a disembodied state as we await the future resurrection. (3) We altogether cease to exist and then get resurrected at the general resurrection.[6]

Jesus' preaching to the spirits in 1 Peter 3 and his meeting with Moses and Elijah on the mount of transfiguration in the Gospels of Matthew (chap. 17), Mark (chap. 9), and Luke (chap. 9) may seem to go against the nonexistence/re-creation view. The reason is that, with respect to the transfiguration, one may think it is simply not plausible that after the meeting between Jesus, Moses, and Elijah, Moses ceased to exist *again* and be re-created at the general resurrection. Moreover, Elijah, on the other hand, was assumed bodily from the earth and, apparently, never ceased to exist a first time. Therefore, in his case at the very least, the nonexistence/re-creation account does not hold at all.

Although it seems that if God created Moses a first time, it would be no problem for God to create Moses a second or third time, I want to grant that the nonexistence/re-creation view is not to be preferred.

5. See ibid., 105.
6. See ibid., 104–8.

And my reason is this: The nonexistence/re-creation account appears to conflict with Scripture and tradition. In particular, as John Cooper has argued, it appears to conflict with orthodox Christian teaching concerning the dual natures of Christ. He was, we believe, one person with two natures, one human nature (as Jesus of Nazareth) and a distinct divine nature (as the Second Person of the Trinity). These natures, as Chalcedon emphasizes, are neither mixed nor separated. The conflict is said to consist in the fact that the death of the human being Jesus results in the separation of the human and divine natures. If the human nature ceases to exist and the divine nature continues to exist, then the two natures are, contrary to Chalcedon, separable. Cooper argues that if the nonexistence/re-creation view is true, then really what we have in the resurrection is no resurrection at all but a *re-incarnation* of the divine nature.

I find this line of argument against the nonexistence/re-creation account persuasive, at least for Jesus. Moreover, if we are going to take the orthodox creeds seriously, then it seems we have to reject the nonexistence/re-creation view insofar as the view conflicts with the tradition's commitment to a doctrine of the communion of the saints, which entails an intermediate state of conscious existence.

With respect to immediate resurrection, Cooper argues that it is ruled out because between his death and resurrection either Jesus didn't exist or, if he continued to exist, he did so in nonbodily form, given the fact that his body was in the tomb during the same interval of time. In other words, immediate resurrection appears to be ruled out, at least for Jesus, on the grounds that Jesus continued to exist (he descended into hell and preached to the prisoners, for example) but his body was in the tomb. Surely, his body could not both be raised and be in the tomb during the same interval of time.

Since it is unlikely that first-century readers would have bought the nonexistence/re-creation/nonexistence/resurrection scheme for Moses, or anyone else for that matter, Cooper suggests that the nonexistence/re-creation view has little going for it. And although both an intermediate state of disembodied, conscious existence and immediate resurrection are consistent with the transfiguration accounts, other New Testament teaching rules out *immediate* resurrection. Therefore, the only plausible alternative, according to Cooper, is the intermediate state of conscious but disembodied existence.

My complaint is simply that Cooper's list of alternatives is not exhaustive. There is a fourth alternative: an intermediate state of *bodily* existence where the body is not yet glorified because it has not yet participated in the resurrection. The question, of course, is how there can be such an intermediate-though-not-yet-glorified body for Jesus when his body was in the tomb. In chapter 3 I discussed in some detail what a body is and what it takes for a body to persist through time. Let it suffice to say here that while I firmly believe that both Scripture and the Christian tradition assert the truth when they (and we) assert that Jesus' body was laid in the tomb, I do not think the New Testament writers made a distinction between an organism (or body) and a corpse. Yet that difference, as I have argued, is an important one. When we attest to the fact that Jesus' body was laid in the tomb, what we assert is that Jesus' corpse (the aggregate of matter that composed Jesus' body) was laid in the tomb. Since the New Testament writers were not interested in making nuanced, philosophical distinctions but rather in communicating the gospel, it is not surprising that they did not make a distinction between a body and a corpse. The important point here is that Cooper presents what he takes to be an exhaustive list of choices. But the list is not exhaustive as it fails to include the view of an intermediate state of *bodily* existence.

In the end, I find the arguments for a dualistic anthropology to be flawed. If the Old and New Testaments do in fact teach that there is an intermediate state of conscious existence, this in no way entails dualism. The fact that we have found dualism taught in the Bible may have more to do with the conceptual context within which we have read it (a context that fails to allow for an intermediate state of *bodily* existence) than what it actually teaches.

The Famous Proof Texts Argument for Dualism

Although I have warned against the practice of pointing to particular texts to settle philosophical questions, I think it will help to consider briefly particular Old and New Testament passages that seem to teach dualism. Surprising as it may seem at first, the passages do not clearly teach dualism and are in fact perfectly compatible with the Constitution View of persons.

> Deuteronomy 6:5: "You shall love the LORD your God with all your heart, and with all your soul, and with all your might."

Isaiah 26:9: "My soul yearns for you in the night, my spirit within me earnestly seeks you. For when your judgments are in the earth, the inhabitants of the world learn righteousness."

Isaiah 55:3 (NIV): "Give ear and come to me; hear me, that your soul may live. I will make an everlasting covenant with you, my faithful love promised to David."

Matthew 10:28: "Do not fear those who kill the body but cannot kill the soul; rather fear him who can destroy both soul and body in hell."

Luke 10: 27: "He answered, 'You shall love the Lord your God with all your heart, and with all your soul, and with all your strength, and with all your mind; and your neighbor as yourself.' "

2 Corinthians 5:8: "We do have confidence, and we would rather be away from the body and at home with the Lord."

2 Corinthians 12:2: "I know a person in Christ who fourteen years ago was caught up to the third heaven—whether in the body or out of the body I do not know; God knows."

1 Thessalonians 5:23: "May the God of peace himself sanctify you entirely; and may your spirit and soul and body be kept sound and blameless at the coming of our Lord Jesus Christ."

The first thing to notice is that in the Old Testament passages the use of the word *soul* does not signal belief in an immaterial substance.[7] The idea is that we are to love and yearn for God with our whole being, with everything we are. And I, of course, affirm the truth of that.

Some of the New Testament passages are a bit more difficult. Notice, however, that none of the New Testament passages explicitly *asserts* a Metaphysical Dualism of soul and body. For example, the 2 Corinthians passages are perfectly consistent with the point I argued for in the last section, namely, that the nonidentity of person and body does not entail that persons are immaterial. Moreover, to the extent that these passages suggest that a person might exist "apart from the body," it does not follow that the nature of that existence is immaterial or nonbodily. Again, like us, it is likely that the apostle Paul did not distinguish between the body or organism of a person and the mass or aggregate of cells that composes the body or organ-

---

7. See ibid., for helpful discussion on this point.

ism. So, to exist in a state that is "away" from the body does not
entail that the state is an immaterial state of an immaterial soul. It
could be a bodily state that includes none of the matter that makes
up the earthly body.

Matthew 10:28 is clearly the most difficult of all the above passages. But notice that the passage is made difficult for a number of
reasons, and once its meaning is sorted out, it is plausible to believe
that it does not assert a dualism of immaterial soul and material body.
The first difficulty is that soul and body are said to be *destroyed* in
hell. However, it is plausible to believe that the destruction of soul
and body in hell spoken of here cannot entail nonexistence. This is
because if both body and soul are destroyed—annihilated—in hell,
then there would be no suffering in hell, for there is no suffering
without a sufferer. Insofar as hell is believed to be a place of suffering, in other words, it entails the existence of a sufferer. Therefore,
destroying soul and body in hell cannot entail the nonexistence of
soul and body in hell. Second, notice that the nature of the afterlife
suggested here is bodily, for if both soul and body can be destroyed
in hell, then there must be a body there to be destroyed.

Despite the difficulties associated with what it may mean to be
destroyed without failing to exist, the meaning of the passage seems
pretty clear: There are some who can bring our earthly existence to
ruin, to an end. But there is another, God, who holds not just our
earthly existence but also our eternal existence in his hands. Do not
fear the one who can bring you to ruin *only* in this life; fear God,
who can bring your life to ruin in *both* this life and the next!

Is Matthew 10, then, unambiguously dualist? Yes and no. The
soul/body division in the Gospel of Matthew seems more in keeping
with a dualism of earthly and heavenly existence. The point of the
passage seems to be that there are those who can destroy us in this
life and another who can destroy in *both* this life and the next. Fear
only the latter, Jesus seems to be telling us in the Gospel of Matthew.
The passage does not seem unambiguously to teach a dualism of immaterial soul and material body, however. The meaning of Matthew
10 seems compatible with the view that the nature of our postmortem
existence is bodily. It is plausible to believe that the dualism taught in
this passage, in other words, is compatible with a non-dualist view
of human nature.

I believe these so-called proof texts have seemed so obviously dualistic partly in virtue of the fact that it has been inconceivable to us

how the verses could assert what is true without entailing dualism. I hope I have been able to show how what these and other Scripture passages assert can be true without dualism being true. But I want to emphasize yet again the following important point. The most important question is not What does *this* text teach about the human person? but How should we understand this text *within the whole narrative of God's Word*? The whole narrative, from creation to new creation, seems to be one of embodiment and materiality.

CONCLUSION

No doubt that as we come to the end of this study I have left many unconvinced. That's okay. If I have succeeded only in getting us to think harder about what we human persons most fundamentally are, then I have succeeded. What I have done in these pages is to offer a philosophical account of human nature that is compatible with orthodox Christian belief. I have provided an answer to the question, What kind of things are we? I have suggested that we are material things, through and through, even if we are not identical with our bodies. I have also attempted to address how this materialist view, the Constitution View, relates to the ethical issues of stem cell research and reproductive technologies such as preimplantation genetic modification. These are important issues for us to think about as Christians. Important as these philosophical questions are, however, they are perhaps not as important as the related question, What is the nature of an authentic human existence? That question, I am convinced, is not best answered by philosophy and metaphysics. That question is best answered by the Bible and by sober theologians past and present. And what they have suggested is that an authentic human existence consists in a fully embodied life rightly lived in relation to God, neighbor, and the rest of the terrestrial world.

Index

abortion, 88–89, 91
  ethical issues of, 84–86, 104–7, 110, 117
Adam, 98
animalism, 16, 54–57, 76, 84, 89–90, 94, 136
animals, humans as, 34–35, 54–55, 136
antimaterialism, of Marcion, 13–15, 95
Apostles' Creed, 13–14, 19
Aristotle, 67
Armstrong, David, 71n9
Athanasian Creed, 19
Augustine, 12

Baker, Lynne, 68
Bible, and philosophical arguments, 138–47
biological body, 13, 16, 65, 69
blastocyst, 100–101, 103, 105, 108, 110
body. See human body
brain, 58–61, 79
Bynum, Carolyn Walker, 121n1

cannibalism, 124–25
canon, biblical, 13–14
causation, 71–75, 128n8
Chalcedonian formulation, 80, 143

Chong, Irina Young, 116n23
Christian beliefs, as concentric circles, 18–20
  and relationality, 73–74
Christian Dualism. See under Dualism
cloning, human, 86, 103, 105, 112, 117, 137
community of parts principle, 76–77
Compound Dualism. See under Dualism
Confessions (Augustine), 12
consciousness, 62, 140–41
  and dualism, 40–42, 44–45
  and materialism, 45, 49–52, 56–64
Constantinople, Second Council of, 25
constituted objects, 65–67, 69, 90, 136, 141
Constitution View, 34, 65–82, 136, 147
  and Christian doctrine, 20–21, 80, 138–39, 144–47
  ethical consequences of, 117, 137
  of human persons, 17, 44, 83–84, 119–20
  objections to, 76–77, 84–87, 94
consumerism, 112
control, in reproductive technologies, 112–15
Cooper, John, 123n2, 139n2, 140, 142–44

corpse, 18, 36, 44, 48, 50–51, 111,
    119–21, 123, 132, 142–44
creation, 74, 95–97, 106–8, 111,
    114–17, 137
creaturely dependence, 96, 106
cryogenics, 111
CV. *See* Constitution View

demiurgus, 13
Descartes, René, 12, 25–35, 38, 55,
    88, 120
disease, curing of, 111–16
Divisibility Argument, 31–33
DNA, 108–9, 113
dominion, meaning of, 81
dualism
    arguments against, 48, 136, 140
    and ethic of life, 85, 94, 117
    and human persons, 14, 26n2, 62–63,
        76, 88–89, 120–27
Dualism
    Christian, 20, 88, 133, 139–47
    Compound, 15, 35–40, 88, 95n16
    Emergent, 15, 40–45, 88, 95n16, 121
    Metaphysical, 83, 87, 145
    Property, 27, 120
    Substance, of Descartes, 15, 25–44
        passim, 80, 85, 88, 95n16, 135
    Substance, of Plato, 15, 23–25

egoism, 112
embodiment, 23, 43–44, 63
    divine affirmation of, 15, 96–98, 108,
        111–12, 115, 117
embryo
    destruction of, 106, 110, 113–14,
        116–17
    ethics of creating, 105–7
    obligation to, 107–11
    and stem cell extraction, 110, 116n23
Emergent Dualism. *See under* Dualism
essential, definition of, 68n4, 80, 135
ethic of life, 83, 85, 88–90, 93–95, 98,
    117, 137
eugenics, 114, 116–17
euthanasia, 85–86

fall and sin, 15, 96–97
fetus, 17, 83–102 passim

first-person perspective, 50, 68, 73–75,
    136–37
fissioning, 132–33
Foster, John, 62n9

Ganssle, Greg, 92–93
gappy view, of resurrection, 123–24,
    128–32
gastrulation stage, 102
gift, and creation, 96, 106–7, 115, 117
God
    as Creator, 59, 91, 95–96
    and human obligation, 94
    as immaterial being, 63, 80
    and incarnation, 95, 97–98
    and resurrection, 92, 97–98, 128–31

Hasker, William, 40–44, 57, 121
hell, 146
Hick, John, 122n2
Hi-Jiang Lu, 116n23
Hudson, Hud, 128–29
human body, 33, 76, 78–79, 121–22,
    144–46
    dualist view of, 24, 26–28, 31–32,
        36–40, 42–44
    materialist view of, 48–54, 65, 67–73,
        75
human community, 88, 91
human persons, 49–53, 79, 88, 91, 93,
    108, 132n11
    Cartesian view of, 26–28, 31–33, 88
    in Compound Dualism, 36–40, 88–89
    in Constitution View, 65, 67–76,
        83–84, 90
    in Emergent Dualism, 40, 43–44, 88
    and materialism, 48, 50–53, 56–59,
        89–90
    Plato's view of, 24

ICC. *See* immanent causal condition
identity
    conditions of, 65–67, 69, 100–101
    and constitution, 56, 65–69, 78, 90,
        122
    definition of, 49, 77n14
    numerical, 29–31, 90, 123, 135–36

person-body, 47–52, 88, 125, 133,
    145
imago Dei, 77, 81–82, 98
immanent causal condition, 72–73,
    127–31, 133
immortality, 24–25
incarnation, 15, 80–81, 95, 97, 114–17
    and ethic issues, 98–99, 107–8, 111,
    137
in potentia, 88, 91
intentional state, 50–51, 52n1, 67–69,
    73, 137
intuition, 86–87
Israel, 96

Jesus
    death and resurrection of, 131, 142,
        144
    divine and human nature of, 15, 80,
        97, 143–44
    as Second Person of Trinity, 19,
        80–81, 97–98, 143
Johnson, Julie, 116n23

kingdom of God, 111–12, 114–15, 137
Klimanskaya, Sandy Becker, 116n23

Lanza, Robert, 116n23
Leibniz, Gottfried Wilhelm, 49, 61–62
life
    definition of, 100, 102
    obligation toward, 84–87, 92
Locke, John, 67

MacKay, Donald, 59n5
Marcion of Pontus, 13–14, 95
Mark, Joel, 116n23
material objects, 36, 72, 76, 96–98
material substance
    and Aquinas, 37, 39–40
    and Aristotle, 67
materialism, 13, 77, 84n3
    of Aquinas, 38–40
    and Emergent Dualism, 41–42, 44–45
    and the ethic of life, 88–89, 94–95
    "nothing but," 12–13, 45–64
    objections to, 84–87, 89–91
McGinn, Colin, 58–63

Meditations on First Philosophy (Des-
    cartes), 12, 28
Meisner, Lorraine, 116n23
mentality, 40–41
mereological sum, 41, 76
Metaphysical Dualism. *See under*
    Dualism
mind, 40–41, 45
miracles, 128
moral beings, 93–94
morality, 59, 88, 113–14, 116–17
Moreland, J. P., 85–89, 92–94
morphogenesis, 102
morula stage, 99–100
multiplying objects, 79–80
multiplying parts, 78
"mysterianism," 58, 61–63

naturalism, 59–62, 89
natural world, 59–60, 63
necessary condition, 70n8, 73–74, 131,
    137
Nicene Creed, 19
non-gappy view, of resurrection, 123–
    24, 132–33
numerical sameness, 30–31, 121–24, 130

obligation
    definition of, 87
    to embryonic stages, 103, 105,
        107–11
    moral, 84–95 passim, 137
Olson, Eric, 55n2
"only x and y" principle, 133
organogenic stage, 102

parent-child relations, 114–16
Paul, 96–97
persistence conditions, 49–50, 56, 70–
    73, 91–92, 120, 125–27, 136
persistent vegetative state, 17, 84, 87,
    91–92
person. *See* human person
personhood, 68n3, 95–98, 108–9
PGD. *See* preimplantation genetic
    diagnosis
Phaedo (Plato), 23
Plato, 15, 23–25

pluripotency, of stem cells, 104–6, 137
preimplantation genetic diagnosis,
    113–14, 116–17
prenatal life, 99–102
principle of persistence. *See* persistence
    conditions
proof texts, biblical, 139–46
properties, 49–50, 75
    in Descartes, 26–27, 120
    and resurrected body, 124, 126, 129
Property Dualism. *See under* Dualism
Ptolemy, 22
PVS. *See* persistent vegetative state

Rae, Scott, 85–89, 92–94
reductionism, 54, 57, 108
Reichenbach, Bruce, 122n2
re-incarnation, 143. *See also*
    resurrection
relationality, 73–76, 81, 98
reproductive technology, 103, 112, 114,
    116–17, 137
resurrection, 92, 123–30, 137–38,
    142–44
    of Christ, 97–98
    and dualism, 18, 42–44, 121–22, 133,
        140
    and moral obligations, 108, 111,
        114–17, 137
    reassembly view of, 123–29
    re-creation view of, 142–43

sameness of bits, 126. *See also* numeri-
    cal sameness
Second Person of Trinity. *See* Jesus
self-referential capacity, 50
Separability Argument, 28–31
Shoemaker, Sydney, 71n9
Simple Argument, 33–34
simples, sets of, 127, 132
sin. *See* fall and sin
soul, 86
    Aquinas's view of, 35–40, 90n12

in Cartesian Dualism, 15, 26–28,
    31–33, 38
in Emergent Dualism, 40, 42–44
human, 63, 86, 121–22, 144–46
of nonhumans, 36n9
stem cells, 103–6, 110
    research on, 103–4, 111–13, 115–17,
        137
Stump, Eleonore, 36nn8–9, 37–39
Substance Dualism. *See under* Dualism
substance, in
    Cartesian Dualism, 26–28, 38,
        120–21
    Emergent Dualism, 40–42
    Thomistic Dualism, 38, 39n16
substantial form, 36–37, 39–40
suffering, 81, 146
supernatural view, 58–60
survival, immediate, 132

theism, 59–60
thinking, 55–56, 79–80
Thomas Aquinas, 35–40, 90n12, 122
transfiguration, 142
Trinity, 74
twinning, 101

unity of consciousness argument, 41–
    42, 44–45, 57. *See* consciousness

Van Inwagen, Peter, 62n10, 63, 125
vanishing weight, 78–79
Verhey, Alan, 14
vocation, 96, 106–7

Ware, Timothy, 19n8

Zimmerman, Dean, 73n13, 128–29,
    132
zona pellucida, 99–101
zygotic stage, 99, 101